Dad Facts

The Funny Book for Dads

Interesting Facts, Quick Stories & Trivia

A Perfect Gift for Dad

BN William

Copyright © 2025 by B N William

All rights reserved. No part of this publication may be reproduced, stored in a retrieval system, or transmitted in any form or by any means, electronic, mechanical, photocopying, recording or otherwise, without the prior written permission of the publisher.

This book is a work of nonfiction. Every effort has been made to ensure accuracy at the time of publication. Some dialogue and details have been lightly adapted for clarity.

For permissions or inquiries, contact: **BNW Publishing**

Ahhhh, The Know-It-All....

Every family's got one. The walking "actually" machine. The uncle who rewrites documentaries from the sofa. The dad who treats pub quizzes like battlefields. The sibling who thinks Google was created purely to back them up. If that's you, then congratulations, you've just found your arena.

This book is a gauntlet of knowledge, stuffed with facts that swing from history's darkest corners to geography's strangest detours, from brain-bending science to true stories so wild they sound made up (but aren't). It's here to poke holes in your "I already knew that" act and see if you can really hold onto that trivia crown.

Inside, we're talking about everything from Hitler's schemes and Cold War spies to Japanese samurai etiquette, the origin of phrases like "spill the beans," and rockstars who thought they were on cocaine but were actually wired on meth for three-day benders. No surrender, no filter, just the kind of facts you can't argue with, no matter how badly you want to.

So go on, know-it-all. Turn the page. Let's find out if you're really the family's trivia champion... or if your crown's about to wobble.

Contents

CHAPTER 01 7

WHY YOU WOULDN'T LAST A DAY IN FEUDAL JAPAN 7

CHAPTER 02 16

HUMAN BODY GLITCHES 16

CHAPTER 03 23

SPACE, THE COSMIC MURDER HOUSE 23

CHAPTER 04 36

THE DICTATOR'S GUIDE TO PEAK CHAOS 36

CHAPTER 05 45

BODY HORROR 101 45

CHAPTER 06 52

SMALL NATIONS, BIG HUSTLES 52

CHAPTER 07 60

ROCKSTAR CARNAGE 60

CHAPTER 08 69

SCRUBBING UP THE PAST 69

CHAPTER 09 77

DRUGS THROUGH HISTORY 77

CHAPTER 10	85
ALL ABOUT NUKES	85
CHAPTER 11	94
EDGE OF THE WORLD	94
CHAPTER 12	101
POISONOUS DELICACIES	101
CHAPTER 13	108
THE ONLY SURE THING BESIDES DEATH	108
CHAPTER 14	116
DEATH IN BULK	116
CHAPTER 15	126
BORDER CHAOS	126
CHAPTER 16	132
WRITER'S BLOCK	132
CHAPTER 17	139
WILD OUTBREAKS OF MASS HYSTERIA	139
CHAPTER 18	146
FAKE IT 'TIL YOU MAKE IT	146
CHAPTER 19	158
BLOOD, ROSES, AND ROTTEN TEETH	158
CHAPTER 20	167
HUMANITY'S LEGAL DRUG HABIT	167

Before you dive in, here's a little gift: scan the QR code and join our FREE weekly newsletter.

Every week you'll get fresh quizzes, mind-bending facts, and hilarious history stories delivered straight to your inbox. It's like keeping the fun of this book going, long after you've closed the cover.

We'll even send you an exclusive peek at our Amazon #1 Bestseller, Shut the Fact Up.

No spam, no boring stuff. Just facts that surprise, delight, and occasionally make you laugh out loud.

Scan the QR code and start your weekly trivia fix today!

Chapter 01

Why You Wouldn't Last a Day in Feudal Japan

"The nail that sticks out gets hammered down."

In feudal Japan, this wasn't just wise advice, it was practically government policy.

The Tokugawa shogunate thrived on order, silence, and knowing your place.

Life was ruled by rituals sharper than a katana's edge: bow wrong and risk beheading, smell wrong in the bathhouse and risk shame, wander without papers and risk jail. The cherry blossoms might have been pretty, but beneath them lay a society where conformity wasn't optional, it was survival.

Samurai Etiquette Would Wreck You

You're standing in front of a samurai, one hand nervously tugging your kimono (if you even managed to fold it correctly), bowing just a bit too shallow, or perhaps speaking out of turn. In feudal Japan, etiquette wasn't simply about being polite, it was about survival.

Samurai were trained killers wrapped in silk and steel, and even the wrong angle of a bow could be seen as disrespect. That wasn't just a social slip-up, that was potentially your last breath.

The Bushidō code, "the way of the warrior", demanded absolute respect, loyalty, and discipline. If you slipped up, heads didn't just metaphorically roll; they literally rolled into wicker baskets. Imagine trying to keep track of all the rules: don't stand taller than a superior, don't touch their sword, don't question an order. For anyone used to casual handshakes and sloppy 'what's up, mate?' greetings, feudal Japan would chew you up and spit you out.

Rice Was the Paycheck

Now forget your cushy salary, your bank transfers, your Venmo. In feudal Japan, wealth was measured in rice.

Samurai, officials, and peasants all lived under the rice economy. Peasants handed over a big portion of their harvest as tax, samurai were paid stipends in rice, and daimyo (lords) measured their power by their rice-producing lands.

Complain your paycheck is late? Congratulations, you just starved for a month. The Japanese unit koku was literally defined as the amount of rice needed to feed one man for a year (about 180 liters). Lords boasting of "10,000 koku" weren't flexing their yacht size, they were showing off how many mouths they could feed (and armies they could support).

Bathhouses, But No Deodorant

Cleanliness, on the other hand, mattered in a very different way. Public bathhouses, sento, were everywhere, and people scrubbed themselves with hot water and rice bran.

Sounds great, right? Except deodorant didn't exist. The sento was often crammed after long seasons of rice planting, the air thick with sweat, steam, and the chatter of neighbors. Bathhouses weren't simply places to get clean; they were buzzing gossip halls where the whole community sized each other up. Every scrub with rice bran was carried out under the watchful gaze of others, and if you cut corners, it wouldn't stay secret for long. The heat, the smell, the lack of privacy, it all turned bathing into a strange mix of hygiene ritual and public performance.

Soap wasn't common in Japan until much later, so instead of foamy suds, you'd scrape and scrub, hoping your neighbors weren't silently judging your technique. And heaven help you if you skipped bath day; personal odor wasn't just unpleasant, it was shameful. For those used to antiperspirant sprays and five-minute showers, feudal hygiene would feel like running a gauntlet in a steam room.

Heads Were Literally on the Line

Samurai carried the right of kirisute gomen, a Japanese phrase meaning "authorization to cut and leave." It was a law that gave samurai permission to kill commoners who insulted or disrespected them.

In practice, even a sarcastic remark or careless slip of the tongue could cost someone their life. To put it in modern terms: in Japan today tipping is considered rude, but back in feudal times the response to showing disrespect might not be a polite refusal, it could be a samurai cutting you down on the spot.

Ninja Paranoia

And then there was the paranoia. Were ninjas real? Yes. Were they everywhere? No. But try telling that to the average villager peeking into the night. Every creak in the rafters, every shadow in the bamboo groves could mean a silent assassin with poisoned darts and grappling hooks.

Ninja weren't magical, but they were terrifying, skilled practitioners of infiltration, disguise, and unconventional warfare. They often came from the lower classes, including farmers or outcasts, and were trained in what was called ninjutsu, a mix of espionage, survival skills, and combat tricks.

Unlike the samurai, who loudly declared loyalty with armor and banners, ninja operated in the shadows. They served daimyo who needed intelligence on rivals, or who wanted sabotage carried out without the stain of honor that kept samurai from doing such dirty work. Some were hired to sneak into castles, set fires, steal documents, or spread confusion before a battle.

For villagers, the thought of unseen killers loyal to powerful lords was chilling. Sleeping on a straw mat in a wooden house without locks, every creak or rustle outside could set nerves on edge. Rumors swirled of black-clad men scaling walls, slipping poison into food, or vanishing into the night. In reality, many ninja disguised themselves as farmers, monks, or merchants, moving quietly among ordinary people. The line between rumor and truth blurred, and whether the sound outside was an assassin or just a raccoon dog rooting around, the paranoia it created was very real. Sweet dreams.

Travel Was Heavily Restricted

During the Tokugawa shogunate (1603–1868), Japan was divided into more than 250 semi-autonomous provinces ruled by regional lords called daimyo, and moving between them required more paperwork than a modern visa application. Commoners needed official permits to travel between these domains, while checkpoints along the roads enforced the rules with the enthusiasm of airport security guards who actually enjoyed their jobs. Wandering without papers could land you in jail or worse, because apparently even taking a scenic route was considered a potential threat to national stability.

The restrictions weren't just bureaucratic busy work, they were deliberate policy designed to prevent rebellion and maintain the rigid social order that kept the Tokugawa in power. By controlling movement, the shogunate could prevent discontented peasants from organizing across regions, stop masterless samurai (ronin) from gathering into dangerous bands, and ensure that everyone stayed exactly where the government wanted them. It's the ultimate example of social control through inconvenience: can't start a revolution if you can't legally travel to the next town to recruit allies.

The system also prevented the spread of dangerous ideas, foreign influence, and economic independence that might threaten the carefully constructed hierarchy. Even the powerful daimyo were required to maintain residences in Edo (modern Tokyo) and leave family members there as essentially well-treated hostages, ensuring their loyalty through honor and the implied threat that rebellion would endanger their loved ones. It was isolation as statecraft, proving that sometimes the most effective prison doesn't need walls, just really aggressive paperwork requirements and the constant fear that your travel documents might not pass inspection at the next checkpoint.

The Class System Had No Chill

Feudal Japan was a rigid pyramid, and climbing it was virtually impossible. Born a peasant? You would die a peasant, rice-taxed and backbreaking.

Born a samurai? Congratulations, but you lived under the Bushidō code and risked death if you dishonored your lord. Merchants, ironically, were near the bottom, despite eventually becoming wealthy, because Confucian (the philosophy developed by the Chinese thinker Confucius, which emphasized social harmony, hierarchy, and respect for traditional roles) values ranked them below farmers (who at least produced food).

"Follow your dreams" wasn't advice anyone gave; your fate was sealed at birth. The only way out was catastrophe: a rebellion, a famine, or some chaos that shook the hierarchy. The Tokugawa shogunate enforced this system with an iron grip.

This kind of rigid structure is alien to many modern societies, but echoes remain. Take India's caste system. Though officially abolished, it still influences opportunity and social mobility in subtle and not-so-subtle ways. Or look at Britain's class system, where the aristocracy once controlled vast power and, even today, accents and schooling can quietly gatekeep jobs and influence. The United States prides itself on being a land of opportunity, yet studies show that economic mobility is harder than in some European nations; being born into poverty often means staying there.

What ties all of these together is the idea of social stratification, which is just a dressed-up way of saying society stacks people like a badly organized Jenga tower. In Edo Japan, the layers were cemented into place with no hope of rearranging, while in our world today, the cement is more like super-sticky chewing gum: you can wriggle a bit, but it clings stubbornly.

The core question is timeless....how much of your life is yours to shape, and how much is doled out the moment you're born? We still wrestle with that, even if the stage has shifted from rice fields to résumés. And for the record, dropping a line like "just grind harder" in Edo Japan wouldn't have motivated anyone, it would've earned you an express ticket out of the rice paddy, courtesy of a samurai's blade.

Blackening Was Fashionable

Married women and noblewomen in feudal Japan dyed their teeth black in a practice called *ohaguro*. The dye was brewed from iron filings dissolved in vinegar, then mixed with tannin-rich gallnut powder to create a shiny black lacquer. It was applied with a small brush every few days, often during evening grooming rituals. Blackened teeth signified maturity, beauty, and marital devotion, while white teeth were linked with youth, wildness, and even animalistic behavior. The custom marked the transition from girlhood to womanhood as clearly as a wedding ring might today.

Ohaguro wasn't only about appearance—it had practical effects. The iron compound acted as a sealant, strengthening enamel and reducing cavities in an era without toothbrushes or modern dentistry. Some samurai used it as well, believing it made them look dignified and fearsome, especially when paired with lacquered armor. The Tokugawa government eventually banned *ohaguro* for unmarried women to maintain strict class and gender roles, fearing blurred boundaries between maidens and married women could disrupt social order.

Chapter 02

Human Body Glitches

Your body is a masterpiece of evolution, billions of cells working in symphony, nerves firing faster than lightning, muscles flexing with hidden hydraulics. Yet for all that brilliance, it's far from flawless. Like a vintage car, it rattles, stalls, and throws up odd glitches that don't quite make sense.

From leftover reflexes to organs with questionable purpose, the body carries reminders of an evolutionary past that sometimes feels more like a programming error than intelligent design.

Charles Darwin and Alfred Russel Wallace might have argued over who first spotted natural selection, but they'd both agree on one thing: our bodies are full of proof that evolution tinkers more than it perfects.

False Alarms and Goosebumps

Step from a steaming shower into a chilly room, jump at a horror film, or feel your chest swell at a song and suddenly your skin bristles with bumps. Sudden temperature changes or a rush of adrenaline trigger the arrector pili muscles at the base of hair follicles, forcing them to contract. In our furrier relatives this raises a coat for insulation or intimidation, but in us it is only a cosmetic ripple of flesh.

The reflex still clings to our emotions. A Beatles track in a dark moment or a movie you have watched more than ten times and still feel in your bones can summon gooseflesh as though the body insists on showing it is moved. Psychologists even joke that replaying the same film endlessly borders on a mild disorder, so maybe consider trying something new next time you want a shiver.

Scientists even have a name for this emotional goosebump response: frisson, from the French for "shiver" or "thrill." It is sometimes described as a skin orgasm, a sudden wave that fuses music, memory, and physiology into a single electric moment. Research suggests this frisson response is linked to the brain's reward system, with dopamine flooding the same pathways activated by food, sex, or drugs. That is why a swelling symphony or a perfectly timed film scene can feel addictive, your brain is literally rewarding you for the thrill.

Tailbone Trouble

At the base of the spine sits the coccyx, a remnant of a vanished tail. It's usually three to five fused vertebrae, and along with the ischial tuberosities, the bony points at the bottom of your pelvis, it forms a tripod that helps us sit upright.

This is why an injured coccyx makes every chair feel like a medieval torture device. Muscles and ligaments of the pelvic floor, vital for bowel control and organ support, hook into this bony stub. In women it can even flex slightly during childbirth to create more space, a detail most male readers might be quietly grateful not to experience firsthand. But its fragility is legendary, falls on the ice, hours of cycling, a bad landing from horseback, even childbirth itself can bruise, dislocate, or fracture it.

Most injuries fade with rest and cushions, though a stubborn few end with a coccygectomy, surgical removal of an evolutionary leftover we can't quite shake.

Nature's Worst Graduation Gift

Wisdom teeth erupt in early adulthood, crowding jaws too small to house them properly. Our ancestors had bigger jaws for grinding raw roots and meat, but as cooking and tools took over, the jaw shrank while the genetic code for third molars stayed behind. They tilt, wedge into bone, or press painfully against nerves, sending millions to oral surgeons.

Before modern dentistry, the eruption of wisdom teeth was seen as a sign of maturity, a final ordeal on the way to adulthood.

The name "wisdom" teeth comes from that moment, a marker of transition even if the pain was less enlightenment and more trial by swelling. Extraction later became a rite of passage in its own right, so common that people often left the dentist clutching their removed molars in a little plastic bag like a grim party favor. Sterilization and biohazard rules have made that practice rare today, but it shows how even oral surgery became a cultural milestone.

The Tadpole Reflex

A hiccup happens when the diaphragm, the muscle that helps you breathe, suddenly spasms and your vocal cords snap shut, making the familiar "hic" sound. Scientists think this may be a leftover from ancient amphibians, like tadpoles, which used a similar reflex to gulp air without letting water flood their lungs.

In humans it no longer has a purpose. Common triggers include overeating, fizzy drinks, alcohol, or even laughing so hard that you swallow too much air. Sudden changes in temperature, like drinking hot soup and then cold water, can also irritate the nerves involved.

Two nerves, the vagus and the phrenic, play a role here. They send mixed signals that confuse the body into repeating this old reflex. It's an evolutionary hangover, a line of code that never got deleted, proving that not every quirk of our bodies is finely tuned for modern life.

Backup with a Bad Temper

The idea of the appendix being useless largely originated with Charles Darwin in the 19th century. In The Descent of Man, Darwin theorized that it was a vestigial organ, a shriveled remnant of a larger cecum that our plant-eating ancestors once used to digest fibrous vegetation. As human diets shifted toward softer, cooked foods, the cecum shrank and left behind what he thought was a purposeless leftover. His theory stuck for over a century and became a standard teaching in evolutionary biology.

However, modern research paints a different picture. The appendix has evolved independently at least 30 times in mammals, showing up in creatures as different as koalas, beavers, and even platypuses.

If it were truly useless and dangerous, natural selection should have erased it long ago. Instead, its persistence suggests an advantage. Scientists now describe it as a kind of safe house for gut bacteria. Its tucked-away location and narrow tube create a refuge where good microbes can survive illnesses that flush the intestines clean, later helping to repopulate the gut after infections like cholera or dysentery.

History also shows how dangerous it can be. For centuries, doctors recognized intense pain in the lower right abdomen but didn't know the appendix was to blame. Only in 1886 did surgeon Reginald Fitz name the condition "appendicitis" and argue for early removal. Before then, treatment often waited until rupture, which was frequently fatal.

Even now, hundreds of thousands face emergency appendectomies every year. Adding to its story, the appendix is packed with lymphoid tissue, part of the immune system that helps produce antibodies, especially in younger years. This makes it more than a spare part: it is both a bacterial backup tank and an immune ally, though one that can turn on you without warning.

The Old Hag Returns

Sleep paralysis locks the body in place even after the mind has woken. People feel pressure on the chest, hear phantom whispers, or glimpse a shadow in the room, a waking dream they can't escape.

Folklore told darker stories of demons and witches, the infamous "Old Hag" squatting on the chest of sleepers. In Japan the experience became kanashibari, a phrase meaning "bound by metal chains," as though a vengeful spirit had you pinned. In Mexico people whisper se me subió el muerto, "the dead climbed on top of me," a chilling image of a corpse pressing down. In Vietnam it is called ma đè, or "ghost pushes down," a name that leaves no doubt about who is in charge.

Among the Yoruba in Nigeria it becomes ogun oru, "nocturnal warfare," a battle fought in the dark between spirit and sleeper. Which sounds most horrifying to you? Personally, I'd put my vote on Japan's vision of being shackled by unseen chains.

Today science calls it a lag between brain and body, a very specific sleep glitch. During REM sleep your brain floods the nervous system with glycine and GABA, chemical paralysis agents that keep you from punching walls while dreaming of fights. But sometimes the wires get crossed.

Your consciousness flickers on like a bulb while your limbs remain dead weight, creating a prison of flesh around a fully alert mind. The ancient terrors suddenly make perfect sense: when you can't move but swear something evil lurks nearby, your brain writes its own horror story to explain the inexplicable. It is part dream, part biology lesson, and all terror.

Chapter 03

Space, The Cosmic Murder House

Space isn't "the final frontier," it's a cosmic murder house with no exits and a thousand ways to die. While NASA's marketing department sells dreams of stellar exploration, the universe has been quietly perfecting its assassination techniques for 13.8 billion years. Every romantic notion about floating among the stars crumbles when you realize that the void doesn't just want to kill you, it wants to kill you in the most creative ways possible.

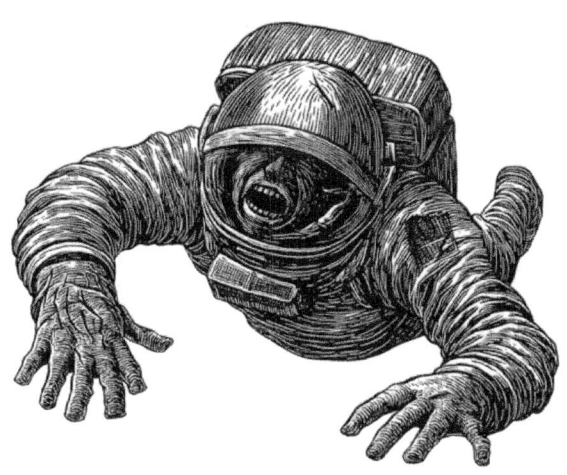

The tech bro marketing brochures never mention that stepping outside Earth's protective bubble is like voluntarily entering a torture chamber designed by a physicist with anger management issues. While Elon's wet dream involves colonies of humans mining asteroids and terraforming Mars, the universe has been quietly perfecting its assassination techniques for 13.8 billion years. These glossy SpaceX presentations, crafted by Silicon Valley types who think disrupting gravity is just another coding problem, conveniently skip the part where space doesn't play fair. It doesn't even play by rules. It simply exists as a vast, indifferent killing field where the laws of physics double as murder weapons and venture capital can't buy you a breathable atmosphere.

The Vacuum Assassin

Exposure to space vacuum triggers a cascade of physiological failures that occur within seconds. The vacuum doesn't create the suction effect popularized by science fiction. Instead, the absence of atmospheric pressure allows gases dissolved in bodily fluids to form bubbles, a condition called ebullism. The air in your lungs expands rapidly, potentially causing pulmonary barotrauma if you attempt to hold your breath.

Consciousness lasts approximately fifteen seconds as oxygen in the bloodstream gets consumed. The boiling point of water drops dramatically in vacuum conditions, causing saliva to bubble on the tongue and tears to vaporize from the surface of the eyes. These aren't effects of temperature but purely pressure-related phenomena occurring at normal body heat.

NASA's vacuum chamber tests have recorded these effects in controlled conditions lasting no more than seconds. Test subjects report immediate pain in their chest cavity as trapped air expands, followed by rapid onset of hypoxia, a condition where an adequate amount of oxygen is not available to the body's tissues or organs, preventing them from functioning normally. The sensation of swelling throughout the body occurs as water vapor forms in soft tissues.

The Apollo 1 tragedy demonstrated how quickly atmospheric conditions can turn lethal. During a routine ground test on January 27, 1967, a spark in the pure oxygen environment of the command module created a flash fire that killed astronauts Gus Grissom, Ed White, and Roger Chaffee in less than twenty seconds. The cabin pressure, far from being absent, was actually 16.7 psi of pure oxygen, a detail that made the fire burn with devastating intensity. The tragedy led to comprehensive redesigns of spacecraft atmospheres and materials, but underscored how marginal the difference between life and death becomes in any space-related environment.

Radiation's Slow Cook

The sun looks friendly from Earth, all golden and life-giving. In space, it reveals itself as a nuclear furnace hurling cancer at everything in sight. Without our atmosphere and magnetic field to deflect the worst of it, cosmic radiation strips through your cells like invisible bullets, shredding DNA with the enthusiasm of a paper shredder.

Solar particle events, essentially radiation storms, can deliver a year's worth of exposure in hours. During the 1972 Apollo missions, a massive solar flare erupted just months after the last moon landing. If astronauts had been caught between Earth and the moon during that storm, they would have returned as walking tumors.

Astronauts on the International Space Station see flashes of light when they close their eyes, cosmic rays literally passing through their eyeballs and triggering their optic nerves. Each flash represents radiation tearing through their brain tissue. They joke about "space sparkles," but each twinkle is cellular damage accumulating like interest on a debt they can never repay.

Long-term Mars missions face an even grimmer calculation. By the time astronauts reach the red planet, they'll have absorbed enough radiation to guarantee cancer. Mission planners don't discuss whether crews will develop tumors, but when and how many.

The Bone Dissolution

Gravity isn't just what keeps your feet on the ground, it's what keeps your skeleton from dissolving. Bones, like muscles, operate on a "use it or lose it" principle. In microgravity, your body decides it no longer needs the structural integrity to fight Earth's pull and begins cannibalizing your skeleton with ruthless efficiency.

Astronauts lose bone density at a rate of 1-2% per month. A six-month mission strips away roughly 10% of their bone mass, equivalent to a decade of aging. Hip bones suffer the worst, becoming so brittle that some astronauts face permanent increased fracture risk. Scott Kelly, after spending 340 days in space, returned with bones so weakened that doctors compared them to those of elderly patients with severe osteoporosis.

The body treats bone calcium like an emergency fund, spending it freely when gravity stops demanding structural support. That calcium doesn't simply vanish, it floods the bloodstream and gets filtered through the kidneys, potentially forming stones that would make urination a screaming ordeal millions of miles from the nearest hospital.

Your spine elongates without gravity's compression, making astronauts temporarily taller but at the cost of severe back pain as vertebrae spread apart like accordions. Some never fully recover their original height after long-duration flights.

Muscle Meltdown

Muscles in space don't just weaken, they revolt. Without gravity to resist, they begin dissolving at an alarming rate. Astronauts can lose 20% of their muscle mass within a week, turning from athletic specimens into something resembling overcooked noodles.

The heart, being a muscle, shrinks too. After months in space, astronauts' hearts become smaller and weaker, struggling to pump blood efficiently when they return to Earth's gravity. Some suffer from orthostatic intolerance, standing up becomes a fainting hazard because their cardiovascular systems have forgotten how to fight gravity.

Exercise machines on space stations aren't luxuries, they're life support equipment. Astronauts spend 2.5 hours daily on specialized treadmills and resistance devices, desperately fighting their bodies' determination to waste away. Even with religious adherence to exercise regimens, they still lose significant muscle mass and strength.

The psychological toll matches the physical. Imagine watching your body systematically dismantle itself while floating in a tin can, unable to escape the process. Every day brings measurable proof that space is winning the war against your biology.

Cosmic Pinball

Space debris moves with velocities that make bullets look sluggish. A fleck of paint traveling at orbital speeds carries the kinetic energy of a baseball thrown at 60 mph. Larger fragments, nuts, bolts, pieces of dead satellites, become hypervelocity projectiles capable of punching through spacecraft walls like paper.

The International Space Station regularly dodges debris, sometimes requiring emergency maneuvers when tracking systems detect incoming threats. In 2009, a defunct Russian satellite collided with an active commercial satellite, creating thousands of new pieces of high-speed shrapnel that will remain hazardous for decades.

Astronauts sleep knowing that their thin aluminum walls provide minimal protection against cosmic billiards. A piece of debris the size of a marble could depressurize their habitat in seconds. During spacewalks, they're essentially naked targets in a shooting gallery where every bullet travels at 17,000 mph.

The Kessler Syndrome looms, a theoretical cascade where collisions create more debris, which causes more collisions, eventually making certain orbital regions too dangerous for human presence. We're already seeing early stages of this phenomenon as space becomes increasingly cluttered with the detritus of human ambition.

Temperature Terrorism

Space doesn't believe in comfortable temperatures. Step into sunlight and you're instantly subjected to 120°C heat that could cook meat. Drift into shadow and you'll experience -150°C cold that makes Antarctic winter feel tropical. There's no gradual transition, no middle ground, just instant thermal shock that would kill you in minutes without a perfectly functioning life support system.

Spacecraft thermal control systems work overtime to prevent crew from alternately roasting and freezing during each 90-minute orbit. A single failure in these systems turns the spacecraft into either an oven or a freezer, both equally lethal.

The Apollo 13 crew experienced this firsthand when their service module failed, forcing them to shut down heating systems to conserve power. The command module temperature dropped to just above freezing, and they could see their breath as condensation coated every surface. They were hours away from the cold becoming fatal when they finally reached Earth's atmosphere.

On the moon, where day and night each last two weeks, temperatures swing from +127°C to -173°C. A single crack in a spacesuit during lunar night would cause instant flash-freezing of exposed skin.

Neurological Chaos

Microgravity doesn't just affect bones and muscles, it scrambles your brain. Without gravity's constant directional reference, the vestibular system goes haywire, causing severe spatial disorientation and nausea that can last for weeks. Astronauts report feeling perpetually upside-down, even with visual cues suggesting otherwise.

Fluid shifts in microgravity cause facial swelling and increased intracranial pressure, leading to vision problems that can become permanent. Some astronauts develop "spaceflight associated neuro-ocular syndrome," experiencing blurred vision and retinal changes that persist long after returning to Earth.

Sleep becomes elusive when your circadian rhythms are disrupted by sixteen sunrises and sunsets per day. The space station orbits Earth every 90 minutes, creating a constant cycle of light and dark that confuses biological clocks evolved over millions of years to expect 24-hour cycles.

Cognitive performance suffers as well. Studies show decreased reaction times, impaired decision-making, and reduced memory function in space. When every decision could mean the difference between life and death, having a brain operating at reduced capacity is particularly ominous.

Solar Fury

Solar flares represent space weather at its most violent, magnetic explosions on the sun's surface that hurl charged particles across the solar system at millions of miles per hour. These storms can disable satellites, disrupt communications, and deliver lethal radiation doses to anyone unlucky enough to be caught outside Earth's magnetic shield.

The 1859 Carrington Event, the most powerful geomagnetic storm in recorded history, caused telegraph lines to spark and catch fire. If that same event occurred today, any astronaut on a spacewalk would likely receive a lethal dose of radiation within hours, enough exposure to guarantee death from acute radiation syndrome. The storm was so intense it delivered what would normally be a lifetime's worth of radiation in a matter of hours.

During major solar storms, astronauts retreat to the most shielded sections of their spacecraft and wait for the radiation to subside. They're essentially hiding in their basement while a nuclear hurricane passes overhead, hoping their shelter holds. The sun's 11-year activity cycle means we're always approaching or leaving peak storm season.

Mars missions face particular vulnerability during the 6-9 month journey, with no possibility of rescue if a major solar storm erupts. Mission planners must either accept the risk of crews receiving potentially lethal radiation doses or develop better shielding technology that currently doesn't exist.

The Unknown Biological Threat

While alien microbes remain theoretical, the possibility of encountering extraterrestrial life carries genuine existential risk. Earth's biosphere has no experience with alien biology, leaving us potentially vulnerable to organisms that might treat human tissue as an ideal growth medium.

The Apollo astronauts faced three weeks of quarantine after returning from the moon, a precaution that seems quaint now but reflected genuine concern about lunar pathogens. We abandoned such protocols once we determined the moon was sterile, but Mars presents different challenges.

Martian soil contains perchlorates, toxic chemicals that would poison Earth-based life but might feed hypothetical Martian organisms. Any human mission to Mars risks exposure to completely new alien chemistry that could prove lethal in ways we can't anticipate.

Even Earth microbes behave unpredictably in space. Bacteria grow faster and become more virulent in microgravity, while antibiotics become less effective. Astronauts face increased infection risks from organisms that would be harmless on Earth but turn aggressive in space's altered environment.

Isolation's Silent Kill

The psychological toll of space travel might prove deadlier than any physical threat. Think of it as The Shining in reverse, instead of being trapped in a haunted hotel, you're locked in a small room with the same few people for months, knowing that outside lies an infinite void that wants you dead, while your only connection to the rest of humanity comes through radio transmissions with increasing delays as you travel farther from Earth.

Mars missions will face communication delays of up to 24 minutes each way, making real-time conversation impossible. Crews will experience complete psychological isolation, unable to receive immediate support during crises or emergencies. It's like being trapped in Interstellar's time dilation scenes, except instead of missing years of your loved ones' lives, you're missing their immediate responses when you desperately need human connection.

Studies of Antarctic research stations, Earth's closest analog to space missions, reveal high rates of depression, anxiety, and interpersonal conflict during long-duration isolation. John Carpenter's The Thing captured this claustrophobic paranoia perfectly, though space adds the extra stress of knowing that escape is impossible and that any critical system failure could result in death. At least Kurt Russell's crew could theoretically walk outside without instantly dying.

The overview effect, seeing Earth from space, initially inspires astronauts, but prolonged separation from the planet can lead to profound homesickness and existential dread. Some astronauts report feeling like they've been exiled from the only world that matters, floating helplessly in a cosmic desert. It's the emotional inverse of Contact's spiritual revelation, instead of feeling connected to the universe, you feel utterly abandoned by it.

William Shatner experienced this psychological whiplash firsthand. The actor best known for playing Captain James T. Kirk took a suborbital flight with Jeff Bezos's Blue Origin in 2021, expecting perhaps to channel some of his character's cosmic optimism. Instead, he gave a tearful and deeply moving interview afterward, describing the "overwhelming sadness" he felt upon seeing space's reality. When Shatner looked at the blackness beyond Earth, he saw "vicious coldness," "dark ugliness," and "death."

This contrasted starkly with his view of the fragile, blue planet below, which he described simply as "life." He felt an intense grief for Earth and humanity, suddenly aware of their cosmic vulnerability. Here was a man who had spent decades pretending to explore the stars, only to discover that leaving Earth's embrace felt less like adventure and more like exile from everything that mattered. Even more ironic: his ride to existential dread was courtesy of another tech billionaire whose space company exists largely to fulfill boyhood rocket fantasies, proving that when venture capital meets the void, the void usually wins the psychological battle.

Chapter 04

The Dictator's Guide to Peak Chaos

Libya wasn't supposed to exist. Like most African borders, it was drawn by European colonial administrators with rulers and wishful thinking, smooshing together three distinct Ottoman provinces, Tripolitania, Cyrenaica, and Fezzan. For most people living there, identity meant tribe, region, or city, not some artificial nation-state invented in Rome and London.

Enter Muammar Gaddafi in 1969: a 27-year-old Bedouin army officer from a nomadic tribe who overthrew King Idris in a bloodless coup and spent the next 42 years trying to turn this colonial patchwork into his personal playground. Despite being largely illiterate when he seized power, he ruled through oil wealth, revolutionary rhetoric, and sheer unpredictability that made Libya a petro-state shaped by one man's increasingly unhinged vision.

Gaddafi was so spectacularly unhinged that he deserves his own category of crazy. Most dictators content themselves with the usual mix of oppression and megalomania, but Gaddafi treated reality like a suggestion and international diplomacy like performance art. He was what happens when unlimited oil money meets complete detachment from consequences, creating forty years of behavior so bizarre that fiction writers would reject it as too unrealistic.

Virgin Bodyguards With Combat Training

Gaddafi surrounded himself with an all-female security detail who had to pass both a firearms test and a virginity exam. The "Amazonian Guard" were required to be virgins, trained in hand-to-hand combat, and dressed in military fatigues paired with high heels during official duties.

Gaddafi claimed this was about female empowerment, though requiring gynecological exams for security positions suggests otherwise. These women served as both bodyguards and PR spectacle, making every diplomatic meeting feel surreal. They were his human shields and performance art rolled into one, trained to kill while maintaining their purity for a man who saw no contradiction in either requirement.

Tent Diplomacy

While world leaders stayed in five-star hotels, Gaddafi pitched a Bedouin tent in their grounds and conducted meetings inside it. He traveled with a custom Airbus A340 featuring a jacuzzi and king-sized bed, then insisted on negotiating in his tent because hotels were too Western and decadent.

In New York for the 2009 UN General Assembly, he tried to pitch his tent in Central Park before settling on Donald Trump's Bedford estate, where local officials issued a stop-work order against the unauthorized desert pavilion on the manicured golf course. In Paris, he erected his tent in the gardens of the Élysée Palace, forcing President Sarkozy to crawl inside for meetings. During his 2009 Rome visit, he commandeered part of Villa Doria Pamphili park, symbolically reversing the colonial power dynamic by making Italian Prime Minister Berlusconi visit him in his tent. Moscow's leaders played along, allowing him to set up in the Kremlin's Tainitsky Garden where Putin came calling.

Foreign leaders had to crawl into his tent for state business, literally lowering themselves to his level while he played the noble nomad. His logistics team transported and erected a luxury tent complex that often cost more than the hotels he was rejecting. It was calculated psychological warfare disguised as cultural authenticity.

The Green Book

Gaddafi wrote a political manifesto called "The Green Book" and made it required reading for every Libyan citizen. This three-volume work claimed to solve democracy by creating "Jamahiriya", direct democracy filtered through his personal philosophy that rejected both capitalism and communism in favor of his "Third Universal Theory."

The book's central argument was that representative democracy is fraud because parliaments and political parties "usurp" the will of the people. His solution involved "people's congresses" that would theoretically give every citizen direct say in governance, while simultaneously abolishing wages to make every worker a "partner" in production. In practice, these congresses were tightly controlled by Gaddafi himself, creating an authoritarian state disguised as direct democracy where money and profit would magically disappear.

The book was taught in schools, plastered on billboards, and treated as holy scripture in a country where disagreeing with the author meant disappearing. Gaddafi genuinely believed he'd written the definitive solution to political organization, economics, and social relations all in one rambling manifesto. Libya became a nation-sized book club where membership was mandatory, dissent was fatal, and the only book on the syllabus was written by the guy who could have you killed for bad reviews.

Nuclear Shopping

For decades, Gaddafi secretly bought nuclear weapons components from Pakistani scientist A.Q. Khan's black market network. He was convinced that having a nuclear bomb would make Libya a major player rather than a small oil-rich state.

The program collapsed in 2003 when he watched America invade Iraq and decided nuclear weapons weren't worth the risk. He voluntarily gave up his entire program in exchange for not being invaded, abandoning decades of work after reading the geopolitical situation correctly for once.

Cosmetic Surgery Obsession

In 1995, Gaddafi secretly flew to Rome for extensive cosmetic surgery, liposuction, a facelift, and hair transplants. The surgeon later claimed Gaddafi also requested breast implants, which was refused even by someone willing to perform the other procedures.

This midlife crisis with a scalpel was driven by his fear that looking older would make him seem less powerful. The man who controlled Libya's oil wealth was apparently defeated by his own reflection, convinced that international diplomacy was partly about appearance management.

King of Kings of Africa

In 2008, Gaddafi hosted a summit of around 200 African kings and traditional leaders, who crowned him "King of Kings, Sultans, Emirs, and Sheiks of Africa." While this title carried no real political power, Gaddafi embraced it wholeheartedly as part of his campaign to unify Africa into a single political entity with himself at its head.

The ceremony was largely seen as political theater, but it perfectly captured his grandiose self-image and continental ambitions. He genuinely believed he could become the leader of a unified Africa, using his oil wealth to fund various African governments and rebel groups in pursuit of influence. His support for armed groups wasn't limited to Africa, he bankrolled organizations from the IRA to Palestinian factions, seemingly more interested in backing anyone who opposed established order than in any coherent ideology. The title became another prop in his ongoing performance as a revolutionary leader who transcended ordinary national boundaries and conventional definitions of state-sponsored chaos.

Fear of Flying

Despite his love of grand international gestures, Gaddafi had an extreme fear of heights that created massive logistical challenges for his diplomatic travel. He refused to stay on upper floors of buildings and wouldn't fly for more than eight hours at a time or over large bodies of water, requiring his custom Airbus A340 to make frequent stops during long-distance trips.

For his 2009 UN visit to New York, he stopped in Portugal before continuing to the United States, turning what could have been a direct flight into a multi-day journey. His phobia meant that international summits required careful planning around his travel limitations, with diplomats having to accommodate a dictator who controlled vast oil reserves but was terrified of being too far off the ground.

The Ukrainian Nurse

Gaddafi was often accompanied by a Ukrainian nurse named Galyna Kolotnytska, described in diplomatic cables released by WikiLeaks as a "voluptuous blonde" who became a key member of his inner circle. WikiLeaks, for those who missed the 2010s media circus, was the organization that published classified government documents leaked by sources like Chelsea Manning, creating diplomatic headaches worldwide by revealing what officials really thought behind closed doors. The cables revealed Gaddafi was "obsessively dependent" on Kolotnytska and couldn't travel without her presence, claiming she was the only person who "knew his routine."

This relationship highlighted Gaddafi's need for constant personal attention and his tendency to blur the lines between professional and personal relationships. Kolotnytska's prominent role in his entourage became another example of how his personal quirks shaped Libya's international image, with foreign diplomats having to navigate the influence of his mysterious Ukrainian companion.

Diplomatic Meltdown at the UN

During his first-ever address to the UN General Assembly in 2009, Gaddafi delivered a rambling 96-minute speech that was supposed to last 15 minutes. He condemned the UN Security Council as a "Terror Council," called for investigations into the assassinations of JFK and Martin Luther King Jr., and dramatically tore a copy of the UN Charter into pieces at the podium.

The speech was a diplomatic train wreck that perfectly encapsulated his disdain for international norms and his belief that established institutions were fundamentally corrupt. World leaders watched in bewilderment as he used the UN's most prestigious platform to attack the very organization hosting him, turning what should have been a routine diplomatic address into performance art that alienated nearly everyone in attendance.

The Single-Color Flag

In 1977, Gaddafi changed Libya's flag to a solid green field, making it the only national flag in the world at the time to be a single, uniform color. The choice of green symbolized his "Green Book" and "Third Universal Theory," turning the country's most recognizable symbol into an advertisement for his personal political philosophy while eliminating any symbols that might represent Libya's pre-Gaddafi history or diverse regional identities.

Reality Catches Up

October 20, 2011, marked the end of Gaddafi's 42-year performance when rebel forces captured him in Sirte, his hometown and final stronghold. The man who had spent decades treating international law as theater, surrounding himself with virgin bodyguards, and forcing world leaders to crawl into his tent was found hiding in a drainage pipe, a decidedly unglamorous end for someone who had built his entire image around grandiose spectacle.

After his capture, Gaddafi was killed by rebel fighters under disputed circumstances, with conflicting accounts about whether he died during crossfire or after being beaten in custody. The precise details remain unclear, but the broader reality was unmistakable: the same unpredictability and disregard for conventional rules that had defined his reign ultimately contributed to his violent downfall.

The man who had rewritten Libya's constitution, redesigned its flag, and declared himself King of Kings of Africa died as many dictators do, abandoned by former allies, hiding from his own people, and discovering that treating reality as performance art only works until reality decides to write the final act itself.

Chapter 05

Body Horror 101

Human bodies weren't designed for adventure. We're basically walking bags of water and gas held together by calcium scaffolding, optimized for shuffling around at sea level eating berries. Yet somehow, we've convinced ourselves we can handle the deep ocean, thin air, zero gravity, and every other hostile environment the universe throws at us. Spoiler alert: we can't. What follows is a scientific tour of how creative the human body gets when you take it places it was never meant to go.

The Bends (Decompression Sickness)

Radiohead named their breakthrough album after a medical condition that leaves people writhing in agony, apparently they felt their usual existential dread needed a more literal interpretation. The bends originally described what happened to burly Irish immigrants in 1870s New York who took jobs digging foundations for the Brooklyn Bridge. Decent pay for straightforward work: descend into a massive iron chamber called a caisson, shovel out mud and rock from the riverbed, then climb back up at the end of your shift. Nobody mentioned they were essentially working inside giant pressure cookers.

The caissons were engineering marvels of their time, pressurised chambers that kept water from flooding in while workers excavated the riverbed. Think of them as primitive submarines, except instead of exploring the ocean depths, they were being driven down into the muck beneath the East River. The deeper they went, the higher the air pressure had to be pumped to match the water pressure outside. Workers would climb down through an airlock, spend their shift breathing air thick enough to make their voices sound like cartoon chipmunks, then climb back up when the whistle blew.

That's when the real trouble started. Men would surface feeling fine, walk a few blocks toward home, then suddenly double over in agony. Their joints seized up like rusty hinges, leaving them writhing on cobblestones, clutching their knees and shoulders. Some couldn't move their arms. Others couldn't feel their legs. The lucky ones just felt like they'd been beaten with cricket bats. The unlucky ones died.

The workers called it "caisson disease," though they had no idea what was actually happening inside their bodies. Neither did the doctors, who prescribed everything from hot baths to laudanum, with predictably useless results. Even Washington Roebling, the chief engineer overseeing the Brooklyn Bridge construction, wasn't immune. After spending too much time in the caissons supervising his workers, he became partially paralysed and had to direct the rest of the construction from his bedroom window, watching through a telescope while his wife Emily effectively took over the project.

The science is brutally simple. Under pressure, nitrogen dissolves into your blood like bubbles in champagne. Surface too quickly, and pop goes the worker. The nitrogen fizzes out violently, forming bubbles in joints and organs that cause agony modern divers avoid by ascending slowly. The caisson workers had no such luxury, they were human bottles of Dom Pérignon, and gravity kept popping their corks.

High-Altitude Hypoxia

Every year, dozens of climbers stumble around Everest's "death zone" like drunken zombies, their oxygen-starved brains struggling to process the simplest decisions. At 8,000 metres above sea level, the air contains roughly one-third the oxygen available at sea level. Your body responds to this shortage with all the grace of a Windows computer running out of memory, everything slows down, critical functions start failing, and eventually the whole system crashes.

The symptoms begin with a polite biological complaint. You might feel a bit winded, perhaps slightly dizzy, like you've had one too many at a wedding. This is your brain's diplomatic way of mentioning it's not getting enough fuel to run at full capacity. As altitude increases, the complaints become less diplomatic. Headaches arrive with the persistence of a door-to-door salesman. Nausea follows shortly after, often accompanied by vomiting that leaves climbers dehydrated in conditions where finding water requires melting snow with precious fuel.

But it's the cognitive effects that turn deadly. High-altitude cerebral oedema causes your brain to swell like a waterlogged sponge, pressing against the inside of your skull. Climbers lose the ability to make rational decisions, often exhibiting what mountaineers call "summit fever", an irrational compulsion to reach the top despite clear signs their body is filing for bankruptcy. They'll abandon safety protocols, ignore weather warnings, and continue climbing even as their coordination deteriorates to the point where walking becomes a drunken stumble.

The death zone earned its name through brutal honesty. Bodies literally cannot sustain life at that altitude for extended periods, regardless of fitness level or experience. Every minute spent above 8,000 metres is borrowed time, with cells throughout the body slowly dying from oxygen starvation. Sleep becomes nearly impossible as the brain repeatedly wakes you up, panicked that you've stopped breathing, like having an overprotective parent who keeps checking if you're still alive. Some climbers develop high-altitude pulmonary oedema, where fluid floods the lungs, essentially drowning them from the inside while they're still conscious and aware.

Commercial airline cabins are pressurised to simulate conditions at around 2,400 metres, high enough that you might feel slightly off if you're sensitive to altitude, but low enough that your body can cope without filing a formal complaint. It's a reminder that even our routine travels require technological intervention to keep us from experiencing the mild versions of what kills climbers who venture too high without enough respect for physics.

Space Eyeballs

Hangovers and zero gravity have more in common than you might expect. Both involve fluid shifting to places it shouldn't be, leaving you feeling swollen, disoriented, and questioning your life choices. The difference is that hangovers eventually go away, while space does permanent damage to your eyeballs.

In Earth's gravity, blood and other fluids flow downward throughout the day, pooling in your legs by evening. Your lymphatic system works constantly to pump excess fluid back up toward your heart, fighting gravity's pull. Remove gravity entirely, and those fluids redistribute like water sloshing in a washing machine, flooding your upper body and head. Astronauts wake up looking like they've spent the night crying at a romantic comedy, their faces puffy and swollen from fluid that normally drains away while they sleep.

The real problem develops over weeks and months. All that excess fluid doesn't just make you look like you've been stung by bees, it increases pressure inside your skull, pressing against delicate structures including the backs of your eyeballs. The optic nerve, which normally sits in a comfortable pocket of cerebrospinal fluid, finds itself squeezed like a tube of toothpaste. The retina, evolved to function within Earth's pressure environment, begins to change shape under the constant squeeze.

NASA has documented this condition in dozens of astronauts, calling it "spaceflight-associated neuro-ocular syndrome," which is medical speak for "space makes your eyes go wonky." Some astronauts return from long-duration flights needing reading glasses for the first time in their lives. Others experience persistent vision changes that never fully resolve. The lucky ones just see slightly blurry; the unlucky ones face permanent alterations to their eyesight that ground them from future missions.

The irony cuts deep for people whose jobs depend on perfect vision. These are test pilots and engineers, people selected partly for their exceptional eyesight and physical condition. Space systematically dismantles these advantages, leaving some of humanity's most capable explorers stumbling around like they need specs they've never worn. It's as if the universe has a particularly cruel sense of humour about human ambition.

Oxygen Toxicity

Pure oxygen sounds healthy, like something you'd pay extra for at a wellness clinic. In reality, breathing 100% oxygen for long periods is like slow-motion poisoning, proof that anything pure enough can kill you.

At normal pressure, pure oxygen brings dry mouth, chest tightness, and a nagging cough. These mild cold-like symptoms hide the danger. Human lungs evolved for air that's mostly nitrogen, and removing it disrupts the balance cells need to function.Under pressure, oxygen turns dangerous fast. Scuba divers risk toxicity when depth raises the oxygen's partial pressure. Early signs can escalate to underwater convulsions, disastrous when you're 40 metres down relying on breathing gear.

Pressurised oxygen spawns' reactive oxygen species that shred cell membranes and DNA. The nervous system suffers most, with sudden violent seizures that can make divers bite through gear or black out entirely. Apollo 1 showed oxygen's fury. Its cabin was filled with high-pressure pure oxygen, making even small sparks lethal. The fire killed astronauts Gus Grissom, Ed White, and Roger Chaffee in under twenty seconds. Modern spacecraft use oxygen-nitrogen mixes to prevent this, a reminder that even life's essentials become deadly when pushed past nature's limits.

Chapter 06

Small Nations, Big Hustles

When your entire country could fit inside a shopping mall, traditional economics goes out the window. These micronations can't rely on manufacturing or agriculture, they need the entrepreneurial equivalent of selling lemonade from a cardboard stand, except instead of citrus, they're monetizing everything from bird poop to internet domains. It's capitalism at its most creative, where geography becomes destiny, and every quirk of history turns into a revenue stream.

Bird Droppings Made Nauru Richer Than Saudi Arabia

Nauru discovered that centuries of bird excrement had turned their island into a phosphate goldmine, making them the richest country per capita on Earth by the 1970s. Picture an island smaller than most airports where everyone lived like oil barons because ancient seabirds had been using their homeland as a toilet for millennia. At their peak, Nauruans enjoyed free healthcare, education, and zero income tax while phosphate revenues poured in at roughly $100 million annually for a population of just 10,000 people.

The wealth was so sudden and overwhelming that the government literally didn't know what to do with it all. They bought a 52-story office building in Melbourne, invested in London real estate, and purchased Air Nauru's fleet of Boeing 737s that flew routes to nowhere particularly profitable. It's like winning the lottery and immediately buying a yacht, a mansion, and a small airline without checking if you actually need any of those things. The cultural shift was equally dramatic, traditional fishing and farming gave way to imported everything, from processed foods to sedentary lifestyles funded by what locals called "the money tree."

The good times lasted exactly as long as the bird poop supply. When the phosphate ran out in the early 2000s, Nauru went from paradise to economic disaster zone, with 80% of the island now resembling a lunar landscape of mining pits and coral pinnacles. The health consequences of the boom years became tragically visible: today, over 94% of the population is overweight or obese, a direct legacy of abandoning traditional diets for imported processed foods during the phosphate bonanza.

Today, they rent detention space to Australia for asylum seekers, earning around $30 million annually. They literally sold their ground out from under themselves, and now 94% of the population carries the physical evidence of what happens when a traditional society gets rich too fast and abandons everything that kept it healthy.

Monaco Bans Locals from Their Own Casinos

Monaco built its entire economy around high-stakes gambling, then banned its own citizens from participating. This bizarre rule dates back to 1863 when Prince Charles III was desperately trying to save his bankrupt principality and decided the best way to prevent locals from gambling away what little money they had was to simply exclude them entirely.

The Monte Carlo Casino opened that same year as part of Monaco's Hail Mary transformation from debt-ridden wasteland into luxury playground. The prince figured if he was going to build his economy on separating rich people from their money, he couldn't risk his own citizens joining the losing side. Monaco's tax system reflects this philosophy: residents pay no income tax because the government makes its money from casino taxes, VAT on luxury goods, and corporate fees from the international businesses attracted by the tax haven status.

Monaco residents get a tax-free lifestyle funded entirely by tourists' gambling losses while being permanently locked out of the source of their prosperity. The locals benefit from being excluded, creating an economic model where being banned from your own country's main industry is actually the best possible outcome.

Liechtenstein Turned Postage Stamps into Foreign Currency

Liechtenstein discovered that designing gorgeous postage stamps and selling them to collectors worldwide could rival their infrastructure budget. These weren't stamps meant for actual mail, they were miniature artworks too beautiful to waste on envelopes, featuring Alpine scenes and royal portraits that philatelists would pay premium prices to never use.

By the 1970s, stamp sales were generating serious national revenue from a product that cost pennies to produce. It's the ultimate luxury goods scam: create something too pretty to serve its intended purpose, then sell it to people who will lock it away forever. Liechtenstein essentially monetized the human impulse to collect shiny things, proving that even in a landlocked Alpine country, you can export beauty to stamp enthusiasts worldwide.

The Marshall Islands Run a Ghost Fleet

The Marshall Islands have 60,000 residents but register one of the world's largest shipping fleets through "flags of convenience", basically renting out their national identity to foreign ships wanting cheaper regulations. It's maritime outsourcing at its purest: massive cargo vessels and oil tankers that have never been within a thousand miles of Majuro fly Marshall Islands flags to avoid their home countries' expensive safety standards and labor laws.

This system exists because of the islands' unique political limbo following World War II. As a former U.S. trusteeship now operating under a Compact of Free Association with America, the Marshall Islands receive financial assistance and defense protection while maintaining sovereignty over their own economic policies. The flag registry offers a form of economic self-sufficiency that complements rather than replaces U.S. aid, creating a revenue stream that requires nothing more than a government office and some very accommodating paperwork. Ships might never visit the islands, but the flag registry brings in steady income without requiring ports, infrastructure, or even seeing the vessels they're supposedly governing.

The economic scale is staggering, flag registration has become one of the country's largest sources of income, often surpassing foreign aid and providing crucial funding for public services like education and healthcare. It's a compelling economic justification for a practice that has serious ethical complexities. Critics point out that this system sometimes leads to accidents and worker exploitation going unpunished, with lax oversight creating conditions where maritime disasters can unfold with minimal accountability. While the notorious 1999 Erika oil spill involved a Maltese-flagged vessel rather than a Marshallese one, it highlighted the dangers inherent in flag of convenience registries where oversight is often more theoretical than practical.

For a tiny Pacific nation facing rising sea levels and limited natural resources, digital revenue from ships they'll never see represents both economic salvation and moral compromise, proving that in the modern global economy, even your flag can become a export commodity.

Tuvalu Accidentally Owns Television

Tuvalu's population of 11,000 stumbled into internet gold when they realized their country code ".tv" was worth millions to broadcasters and streaming platforms worldwide. What started as a random assignment of two letters based on their country name became roughly 10% of their government revenue, proving that sometimes the best business strategies are pure accidents.

GoDaddy handles the technical side while Tuvalu collects royalties from everyone who wants a domain name that screams "media company." For a nation facing rising sea levels and limited natural resources, accidentally owning the internet's most valuable three-character combination is like winning the digital lottery. They're literally selling virtual real estate that doesn't exist physically, making money from domain names while their actual land might disappear underwater.

Kiribati Sells the Future

Kiribati pulled off one of history's most audacious geographical power moves by literally moving time itself to create a tourism marketing opportunity. In 1995, the nation of 33 coral atolls scattered across the Pacific convinced the world to shift the International Date Line eastward, ensuring that their uninhabited Caroline Island would be the first place on Earth to greet the new millennium on January 1, 2000. They renamed it "Millennium Island" and suddenly had a unique selling proposition that no other country could match: the exclusive rights to tomorrow.

This wasn't just millennium fever marketing, it was economic strategy disguised as calendar manipulation. The country leveraged this "first in time" status to attract lucrative licensing deals and international attention to their vast Exclusive Economic Zone, a massive stretch of ocean 14 times the size of California that most people had never heard of. Kiribati transformed from an overlooked collection of atolls into the gatekeeper of global tomorrow, proving that sometimes the best business plan involves convincing everyone else to change their clocks.

The real hustle lies beneath the waves. Kiribati's primary revenue source is now selling fishing licenses to other nations' fleets, monetizing an ocean territory that dwarfs their tiny land mass. By controlling access to some of the Pacific's richest fishing grounds, they've turned geographical isolation into economic leverage, foreign vessels pay millions annually for the privilege of harvesting tuna from waters that belong to a country most people couldn't locate on a map.

It's a poignant irony that cuts deep: a nation on the front lines of climate change has built its economy around monetizing the very ocean that threatens to swallow it whole. While Kiribati sells fishing rights and markets itself as the first place to see each new dawn, rising sea levels continue to erode their coral atolls, making them potentially the first country to disappear entirely beneath the waves. They're literally selling the future while racing against time to ensure they have one.

Chapter 07

Rockstar Carnage

Rock history isn't tidy, it's messy, loud, and sometimes downright unhinged. The following moments aren't just performances, they're explosions of chaos and creativity that rewrote what it meant to step on stage. These are the nights when guitars burned, voices cracked, fists flew, and legends were born.

Dylan Goes Electric

At the 1965 Newport Folk Festival in Rhode Island, Bob Dylan shocked his audience by walking on stage not with his familiar acoustic guitar and harmonica, but with a shiny Fender Stratocaster and a full electric band. For folk traditionalists, who prized acoustic authenticity and saw electricity as the language of commercial pop, this felt like heresy. Cries of "sellout" echoed, and the booing was as loud as the amplifiers.

Yet this uproar marked a seismic shift. It was the birth of folk-rock. The Stratocaster, a model famous for its crisp tone and used by rockers like Buddy Holly, symbolized Dylan's new sound, blending poetic lyricism with the raw power of rock instrumentation. The moment signaled the end of folk purity and the beginning of a new era, one where electric guitars could carry protest songs, love ballads, and social commentary with equal force. It connected Dylan to the cultural upheavals of the 1960s, as music itself was becoming louder, bolder, and more politically charged.

Jimi Hendrix Burns His Guitar

Hendrix didn't just play guitar, he made it an offering. At the Monterey Pop Festival, he closed his set by kneeling before his Fender Strat, soaking it in lighter fluid, and coaxing flames with a few ritualistic hand waves before setting it ablaze.

The crowd, already stunned by his teeth-playing and behind-the-back solos, watched slack-jawed as Hendrix smashed the smoldering remains against the stage. Some thought it was insanity, others genius. In truth, it was both. Hendrix turned an act of destruction into one of creation. A new image of what rock could be.

Nirvana Unplugged, Cobain's Candlelit Funeral

When MTV invited Nirvana for its acoustic "Unplugged" series, most expected stripped-down versions of "Smells Like Teen Spirit" or "Lithium." Instead, Kurt Cobain leaned into his darker instincts. Surrounded by lilies, black candles, and funeral-like drapery, Nirvana played covers by obscure artists like Lead Belly and the Meat Puppets. It was raw, fragile, and eerily prophetic.

Cobain's crackling voice and mournful stare made the whole set feel like a wake, months before his death. Fans expecting a greatest-hits singalong got a haunting requiem instead. The performance has since become one of Nirvana's most beloved recordings, proving you don't always need distortion to blow minds, just guts, grief, and a cardigan that would later sell for over $300,000.

Ozzy Osbourne and the Bat Incident

In 1982, during a concert in Des Moines, Ozzy Osbourne spotted what he believed to be a harmless rubber toy hurled onto the stage by an enthusiastic fan. Without hesitation and with his usual theatrical bravado, he scooped it up and clamped his teeth down, only to realize with horror that it was a very real, very dead bat.

The audience gasped, some cheering in disbelief while others recoiled in shock, as Ozzy quickly spat it out. The stunt turned into a genuine health scare, forcing him to rush to the hospital for a grueling series of rabies shots, painful injections administered over the course of weeks.

Fans later joked that the only true merch you could get from that tour was a signed vaccination card, and unbelievably, some even did manage to get him to autograph their rabies paperwork. The surreal medical ordeal somehow fed perfectly into his legend.

After all, this was the same frontman of Black Sabbath, the band credited with birthing heavy metal by fusing Tony Iommi's brutally down-tuned riffs, Geezer Butler's ominous basslines, Ozzy's eerie vocals, and Bill Ward's pounding drums into something darker than anything rock had ever known. Iommi's own accident, losing his fingertips in a factory mishap, forced him to invent prosthetic thimbles and detune his guitar, a twist of fate that created the heavy, doom-laden sound that became the genre's blueprint.

In this light, Ozzy gnawing on a bat and surviving a string of rabies shots was less a one-off fiasco and more a bizarre extension of heavy metal's origins. Aaccidents, pain, and a little bit of unholy luck turned into music history. RIP to the legend himself, and, in darkly comic fashion, RIP the bat too.

The Who and the Substitute Drummer

Keith Moon, infamous for his wild lifestyle, collapsed on stage in San Francisco in 1973 after taking too many tranquilizers. Instead of cancelling, The Who pulled a 19-year-old from the audience named Scott Halpin to finish the set on drums. Few fans can say they literally became part of The Who for a night.

Oasis and the Meth Mishap

The infamous meltdown came on September 29, 1994, at the Whisky a Go Go in West Hollywood, California. Oasis had partied the night before and, in an act of staggering misjudgment, mistook crystal meth for cocaine.

Meth is a stimulant far stronger and longer lasting than cocaine, and the band paid for the error the next evening. The performance was so incoherent that Noel Gallagher later called it the "worst gig of our lives." Liam Gallagher hurled insults at the American crowd, picked fights mid-set, and at one point even clocked Noel in the head with a tambourine.

After the gig, Noel vanished. He took the tour float, the band's travel cash, and his passport, and fled to San Francisco, staying with a woman named Melissa Lim he had recently met. Out of this bizarre exile came the reflective ballad "Talk Tonight," inspired by Lim convincing him to return. Oasis's manager Marcus Russell and reps from Creation Records eventually tracked him down and persuaded him back on tour, though the Gallagher brothers had to be kept apart for the rest of that leg.

The walk-off left the band in shambles, but with hindsight it reads almost like a dark comedy. Who else but Oasis could turn a meth mix-up, a tambourine assault, and a disappearing guitarist into a hit single and a legendary feud? Today, decades later, the bitterness is mostly blurred. The brothers still exchange barbed words in interviews, but under the banner of the Oasis 2025 Tour they are back together on stage, selling out arenas worldwide, proof that even meth absurdities and family fistfights can't dent the band's enduring myth.

20 Minutes That Stole the Show

On July 13, 1985, Queen took the stage at Wembley Stadium for the Live Aid concert. Their 20-minute set was carefully designed as a string of their biggest anthems, from an abbreviated "Bohemian Rhapsody" and "Radio Ga Ga" to "Hammer to Fall," "Crazy Little Thing Called Love," and finally the one-two punch of "We Will Rock You" and "We Are the Champions." Organizer Bob Geldof had warned bands not to get clever and just play the hits, turning the day into a kind of global jukebox, and Queen nailed it.

Mercury's famous "Ay-Oh" call-and-response wasn't rehearsed, just an improvised vocal warm-up that instantly became one of the defining moments of the entire concert. Unlike many acts who winged it, Queen rehearsed for two full days beforehand to make sure their medley would land perfectly within the strict time limits. The preparation showed: they sounded tight, polished, and utterly commanding.

Other musicians noticed. Elton John reportedly rushed up afterwards and quipped, "You bastards, you stole the show." And he wasn't alone, critics and peers alike agreed that Queen had delivered the definitive performance. With 80,000 at Wembley and a staggering 1.9 billion watching live across 110 countries, the set wasn't just a concert, it was a broadcast that demonstrated the unifying, global power of rock music. Today it is still remembered as one of the greatest live performances.

Woodstock's Evil Twin, Altamont Apocalypse

What was pitched as "Woodstock West" quickly turned into a cautionary tale about mixing rock, drugs, and motorbike gangs. To understand the nickname, Woodstock had been the legendary 1969 festival in upstate New York where nearly half a million people gathered for three days of peace, music, and mud-splattered love-ins.

Altamont, by contrast, was organized in large part by the Rolling Stones and their management as a way to cap their U.S. tour with a free concert. Their involvement was central, they chose the site, set the date on short notice, and controversially approved using the Hells Angels for security. That decision, meant to echo Woodstock's "peace patrol," instead set the stage for disaster.

It became the symbol of the hippie dream, no violence, just flower crowns and endless guitar jams. By contrast, Altamont Speedway hosted far fewer people but carried the weight of expectation to be its West Coast twin. Instead, the Rolling Stones hired the Hells Angels for security, paying them in beer, because what could possibly go wrong?

The answer: everything. Chaos erupted as the Angels clashed with fans. During the song "Under My Thumb," a young man named Meredith Hunter pulled out a pistol in the crowd. One of the Hells Angels stabbed him to death in plain view of the stage. The concert became infamous overnight. Journalists called it the grim bookend to the 1960s' so-called "peace and love" dream, the idea that music festivals could magically stay safe, loving, and communal. In reality, Altamont showed how quickly things could spiral when poor planning and bad security mixed with drugs, booze, and tens of thousands of people.

Bowie Kills Ziggy

Fans packed London's Hammersmith Odeon, expecting another glitter-drenched night with Ziggy Stardust, Bowie's alien rock messiah. Instead, Bowie dropped a bombshell mid-show: "Not only is this the last show of the tour, but it's the last show we'll ever do." Gasps echoed through the venue. Some thought Bowie was quitting music altogether.

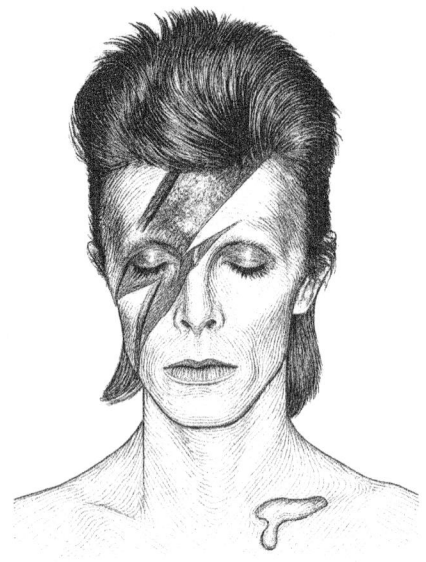

In reality, he was just killing off Ziggy, the persona that had made him a star but was threatening to consume him. Bowie reinvented himself countless times afterward, Thin White Duke, Berlin-era minimalist, pop megastar, but Ziggy's funeral onstage proved his greatest magic trick: he could end one universe and start another with a single sentence. Fans may have cried, but Bowie probably thought mission accomplished, aliens abducted.

Chapter 08

Scrubbing Up the Past

For much of human history, cleanliness was more fantasy than fact, we weren't bathing in glory, we were simmering in grime and masking it with perfume. The past reeks of questionable hygiene choices that make modern germaphobes weep into their hand sanitizer. From royal toilet attendants to Viking soap rituals and even crocodile-dung contraceptives, hygiene's history is a catalogue of oddities that proves humans have always been creative problem-solvers, even when the problems were entirely self-created and the solutions were deeply questionable.

Be warned: you may never swish mouthwash with the same innocence again.

Louis XIV's Laundry Routine Was His "Bath"

The Sun King earned his title by casting himself as France's blazing center, with courtiers obliged to orbit like reluctant planets around a monarch who apparently believed soap was optional equipment for royalty. While the claim that Louis bathed only twice in his entire life is likely an exaggeration designed to scandalize later generations, the truth isn't much more reassuring, he bathed rarely and with great reluctance, viewing the process as medicinal treatment rather than regular maintenance, like taking your car to the shop only when smoke starts pouring from the engine.

Louis's daily "cleansing" ritual was a masterclass in creative problem-solving that avoided actual water contact. Every morning, he had his head and face washed with a special mixture of alcohol and spices while his body was simply dabbed with a wet cloth soaked in perfume, essentially a medieval wet wipe experience for the most powerful man in Europe.

The real act of purification was the rigorous daily changing of linen shirts and stockings, which were treated as filters for impurities and sweat. Fresh linen was considered so effective at absorbing bodily contamination that wearing a clean shirt was literally seen as purification, a belief that would make modern textile scientists either laugh or cry. The medical establishment of the time reinforced these practices with the authority of people who had never heard of bacteria. Doctors warned that water opened the body's pores to disease, making bathing a potentially lethal activity rather than a hygienic one. This created a society where perfume wasn't enhancement, it was survival equipment. Louis's personal perfumer, Maître Fargeon, created custom scents for the king and court using astronomical amounts of fragrance, turning Versailles into what was essentially a luxury air freshener factory disguised as a palace. The result was an aristocracy that looked immaculate in their silk and jewels but smelled like a music festival on the fourth day, if that festival had access to premium French cologne instead of portable toilets.

Vikings Were Grooming Trendsetters

Contrary to their brutish Hollywood image, Vikings were the metrosexuals of medieval Europe, bathing once a week and carrying grooming kits that would make modern travelers jealous.

This weekly bathing schedule was such a shocking luxury compared to their medieval neighbors that it probably counted as showing off, like driving a Tesla through a horse-and-buggy convention. Their soap, made from animal fat and ash, was as harsh as their raids, capable of stripping skin as efficiently as rust off a sword, but at least they were committed to the process. Viking grooming kits were sophisticated affairs crafted from bone and antler, containing tweezers, combs, and ear spoons that showed a practical concern for hygiene extending far beyond basic appearances.

Archaeological evidence from graves and settlements provides tangible proof of these fastidious habits, suggesting that Vikings packed grooming supplies with the same care modern people pack phone chargers. The word for Wednesday in many Germanic languages traces back to Odin, who was associated with cleanliness among his many divine responsibilities, creating a linguistic connection between their weekly bathing habit and their most important deity. This devotion to grooming wasn't vanity alone, it was strategic social and political investment with measurable returns. A clean, well-kept Viking could strike more favorable trade deals and win over potential allies, proving that good hygiene has always been good business.

Anglo-Saxon chroniclers grumbled that Viking men were dangerously attractive to local women, their neat hair and polished beards putting local suitors to shame in what might be history's first recorded complaint about immigrants having better grooming standards.

The Royal Bum-Wiper Was a Power Position

Henry VIII's Groom of the King's Close Stool, and yes, that was the official title, wasn't a lowly servant but one of the king's most trusted advisors. The term "Close Stool" referred to a portable toilet shaped like a stool or cabinet, adding a layer of formal absurdity to a role that transformed bathroom attendance into high-stakes political theater.

This unfortunate courtier literally wiped the king's backside and provided daily health reports based on the quality of Henry's "royal output," creating a job description that combined personal care, medical monitoring, and intelligence gathering in ways that would make modern HR departments question their career advancement policies. The Groom served as both intimate attendant and personal health monitor, observing the king's bowel movements to provide daily reports on the monarch's health and diet to his doctors. This wasn't just scatological record-keeping, it was vital medical intelligence at a time when understanding royal intestinal patterns could mean the difference between effective treatment and watching your monarch die from preventable digestive issues.

The role's political influence extended far beyond bathroom duties, with the Groom often acting as private secretary, confidant, and gatekeeper who controlled access to the king and filtered information reaching the royal ear. Sir Henry Norreys, one of Henry's most trusted Grooms of the Stool, wielded influence that made him essentially a cabinet minister whose office happened to be a bathroom. His eventual fall from grace, he was executed in 1536 on charges of adultery with Anne Boleyn, was considered a major political earthquake that sent shockwaves through the Tudor court, demonstrating how a position that began with wiping royal bottoms could evolve into wielding the kind of intimate knowledge and access that could influence royal policy and reshape kingdoms.

George Washington's Dentures Were Human Too

Forget the wooden teeth myth that somehow makes America's founding father sound like a hand-carved nutcracker, Washington's dentures were far more disturbing than any fairy tale.

His dental appliances were constructed from hippopotamus ivory, cow teeth, gold wire, and human teeth, often purchased from poor individuals or extracted from enslaved people, creating a smile that was less presidential gleam and more Frankenstein mosaic of economic desperation and racial exploitation.

The human teeth component reveals the grim realities of 18th-century healthcare, where dental solutions depended on a marketplace of poverty and powerlessness that would make modern medical ethicists reach for their strongest antacids. Each time Washington posed for a portrait, painters captured a grim collage of ivory, bone, and stolen humanity held together by gold wire and springs that caused constant pain and inflammation.

The dentures were a constant source of physical agony that contributed to Washington's famous grimaces in portraits and paintings, those stern, tight-lipped expressions weren't just presidential gravitas, they were pain management techniques for dealing with dental appliances that clacked like bad carpentry and required constant adjustment. The father of a nation delivered speeches about freedom and democracy through a mechanical jaw that represented some of the least free aspects of American society, creating an irony so sharp it could probably cut through hippopotamus ivory.

Crocodile Poop as Contraception

Ancient Egyptian women used crocodile dung mixed with honey as barrier contraception, proving that humans have always been willing to get creative when it comes to family planning, even if creativity involves ingredients that would make modern pharmaceutical companies reconsider their career choices.

The specific recipe, detailed in papyrus medical texts, called for a paste of crocodile dung, honey, and natron, a type of salt, inserted as a pessary that was probably more effective at preventing romance than preventing pregnancy.

The choice of crocodile excrement wasn't entirely random; these sacred animals held divine significance in Egyptian religion, which may have made their waste seem more potent and mystically powerful than regular animal droppings. It's the ancient equivalent of buying supplements because they have a celebrity endorsement, except the celebrity was a reptilian deity and the supplement was literally crap.

This wasn't an isolated oddity but part of a broader pattern of experimental ancient medicine where hope often outweighed scientific understanding. Greeks used olive oil or cedar oil as spermicides, while various cultures employed acidic fruit pulps, creating an international marketplace of questionable gynecological advice.

Roman Public Toilets Were Social Hubs

In ancient Rome, public latrines weren't private stalls but long marble benches with keyhole-shaped openings, lined up side by side without partitions. Dozens of people could relieve themselves shoulder to shoulder while chatting about politics, gladiator gossip, or dinner plans. Beneath the benches ran a continuous stream of water to carry away waste, while another trough of clean water in front held sponges on sticks, *tersoria*, used communally for wiping.

These sponge sticks were rinsed between uses, but not sterilized, meaning everyone effectively shared the same ancient toilet brush. Roman engineers even designed some latrines with heated floors, making them surprisingly comfortable for leisurely socializing.

Archaeological evidence from Ostia and Pompeii shows lavish mosaics decorating the walls, suggesting they were meant to impress guests as much as serve a function. For Romans, relieving oneself was less a solitary task and more a networking opportunity, business deals and Senate alliances were literally forged over the sound of running water and echoing splashes.

Chapter 09

Drugs Through History

History's medicine cabinet reads like a pharmacist's fever dream mixed with a chemistry experiment gone wrong. For thousands of years, humans have been mixing, smoking, drinking, and injecting whatever they could find, convinced that this time they'd discovered the miracle cure. Romans used lead-sweetened wine for everything from headaches to hangovers, while medieval Europeans swore by mercury treatments that probably killed more patients than the diseases they were supposed to cure.

The pattern never changed: someone discovers a new substance, declares it revolutionary medicine, markets it to desperate people, then quietly retreats when the body count gets embarrassing. History doesn't repeat, but it certainly rhymes, the same cycle that gave us laudanum and heroin as "safe" painkillers delivered us OxyContin and the opioid crisis, while synthetic opioids like fentanyl prove we're still writing verses to the same deadly song.

Medieval Wonder Drug Was Sixty Ingredients of Nonsense

Medieval Europe's miracle cure was theriac, a supposed antidote that contained over sixty ingredients including viper flesh, honey, cinnamon, and opium. Galen, the Greek physician whose medical advice shaped centuries of European medicine, claimed theriac improved with age like fine wine, six-year-old batches were considered premium vintage.

Apothecaries sold this kitchen-sink concoction as both medicine and poison protection, though it was essentially expensive placebo in a jar. Kings, merchants, and peasants all gulped it down, convinced they were drinking bottled immortality. The recipe was so complex that preparing authentic theriac became a public spectacle, with officials overseeing the process to prevent fraud. Medieval people would line up to buy snake-meat medicine because a famous doctor from centuries earlier had endorsed it, the power of celebrity endorsement transcending both death and common sense.

Cannabis Was Everywhere Before It Wasn't

Cannabis has been threading through human civilization since ancient Egypt, where medical texts from 2000 BCE recommended mixing it with honey to "cool the uterus." The Scythians built sweat lodges specifically for getting high, tossing hemp seeds on hot stones and inhaling the vapor while "howling with joy," according to Herodotus, basically the world's first documented hotbox session.

Romans prescribed it for gout and earaches, Vikings carried hemp seeds for trade, and medieval Europeans used it for childbirth pain until Pope Innocent VIII condemned it in 1484 as an "unholy sacrament." Colonial American farmers were legally required to grow hemp, and it was sometimes accepted for tax payments, imagine explaining to the IRS that your crop literally went up in smoke.

Cannabis was so ubiquitous across cultures and centuries that finding a civilization that didn't use it is harder than finding one that did. The plant kept cropping up everywhere, literally and figuratively, as medicine, ritual, fiber, and currency before modern prohibition turned it into contraband. History itself seems to have had a serious case of the munchies when it came to hemp, consuming it in every possible form across every possible culture until someone decided to harsh everyone's millennium-long buzz.

Coffee Nearly Got Banned for Being Too Fun

When coffee arrived in the Ottoman Empire during the 1500s, religious authorities tried banning it because they believed the dark brew stirred sinful thoughts. The logic was that anything that made people feel energetic and social must be leading them away from proper devotion, essentially treating caffeine like a gateway drug to having too much fun.

Coffee won the cultural war anyway. Coffeehouses exploded across Ottoman cities, becoming centers of gossip, politics, and poetry where people gathered to drink, debate, and stay awake way too late. What started as forbidden fruit quickly became the morning fuel of empires. Coffee proved that once people discover something that makes them feel better about being conscious, no amount of religious prohibition can stop them from brewing it.

The discovery story itself reads like folklore, because that's exactly what it is. According to Ethiopian legend, a goat herder named Kaldi noticed his goats acting unusually energetic after eating certain red berries. Instead of worrying about hyperactive livestock, he tried the berries himself and felt the same buzz. Monks at a nearby monastery heard about this magical fruit, brewed it into a drink, and found they could stay awake for evening prayers without nodding off. Whether Kaldi actually existed or this tale was invented to explain coffee's origins, the story perfectly captures humanity's relationship with stimulants: we literally follow the lead of any creature that seems to be having more fun than us.

Switzerland Accidentally Created the Sixties

In 1938, Swiss chemist Albert Hofmann was trying to develop a circulatory stimulant at Sandoz Laboratories, something practical for heart patients, not cosmic fireworks for hippies. He synthesized LSD-25 but shelved it for five years when initial tests showed no promising medical effects. In 1943, he accidentally absorbed some through his skin while handling the compound and experienced the world's first acid trip, proving that the most profound discoveries often happen when you're definitely not looking for them.

Three days later, Hofmann intentionally took 250 micrograms and rode his bicycle home while convinced his neighbor was a witch and his furniture was alive. April 19, 1943, became "Bicycle Day", the unofficial birthday of psychedelia. What started as a failed heart medication became the chemical foundation of counterculture, because apparently the universe has a sense of irony about Swiss precision meeting cosmic chaos.

The CIA got interested first, dosing unwitting subjects in MK-Ultra experiments during the 1950s before LSD escaped government labs and found its way to artists, writers, and eventually the general public. Hollywood embraced it through figures like Cary Grant, who credited LSD therapy sessions with improving his mental health, while musicians from The Beatles to Jimi Hendrix turned psychedelic experiences into chart-topping albums.

The drug's influence wasn't always positive, Charles Manson used LSD to manipulate his followers, proving that mind-altering substances amplify whatever intentions people bring to them, whether creative or destructive.

Not to go all Alex Jones here, but when government mind-control experiments accidentally create both Sgt. Pepper's and cult murders, maybe laboratory oversight could use some work.

Magic mushrooms, containing the related compound psilocybin, followed a similar path from indigenous ritual use to scientific research to recreational prohibition. The pattern repeats: what starts in laboratories often ends up redefining entire generations, whether the scientists intended it or not.

WWII Soldiers Fought on Crystal Meth

Nazi Germany fueled the Blitzkrieg with Pervitin, essentially crystal meth packaged in chocolate bars and sold as an everyday pick-me-up. By 1940, over 35 million tablets were distributed to German soldiers under an official "Stimulant Decree," earning nicknames like "Tank Chocolate" and "Stuka Tablets." The German military had discovered the pharmaceutical equivalent of unlimited overtime, except the side effects included psychosis.

Soldiers took 2-4 pills daily to skip sleep, ignore hunger, and maintain the chemically induced fearlessness that generals initially praised. Tank crews drove through nights and pilots flew marathon raids while completely wired. Future Nobel Prize winner Heinrich Böll wrote desperate letters from the front begging his family to send more pills to survive the crashes. The drug worked until it didn't, side effects included paranoia, psychosis, and soldiers seeing enemies in potato fields. The German command eventually realized their "miracle pill" was destroying judgment and health, but by then addiction was widespread and the damage was done. Once again, what seemed like pharmaceutical innovation became a cautionary tale about the gap between laboratory promises and battlefield reality.

Bayer Marketed Heroin as Children's Cough Medicine

In 1898, Bayer pharmaceutical company proudly launched heroin as a "non-addictive" wonder drug, marketing it in syrups and lozenges specifically for children's coughs. The company's chemists genuinely believed they'd created a safer alternative to morphine, promoting heroin as medicine that delivered pain relief without the addiction risks.

The marketing campaign was a stunning success, until patients started craving increasingly larger doses and doctors realized they'd created an epidemic instead of a cure. Within a decade, Bayer quietly pulled heroin from pharmacy shelves, leaving behind one of medical history's most catastrophic product launches. It's the pharmaceutical equivalent of marketing cigarettes as lung medicine, except heroin was actually supposed to be the healthy option.

Chapter 10

All About Nukes

"If you're holding the biggest stick in the room, people tend to listen, unless, of course, they're also holding sticks that glow in the dark."

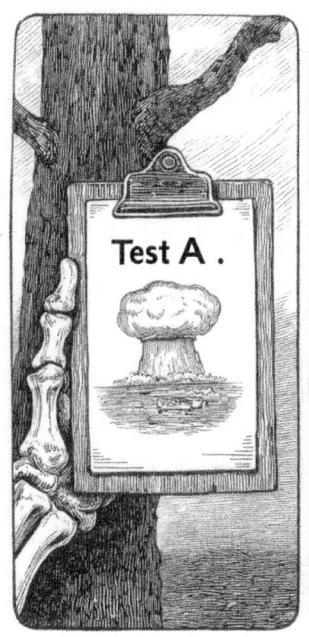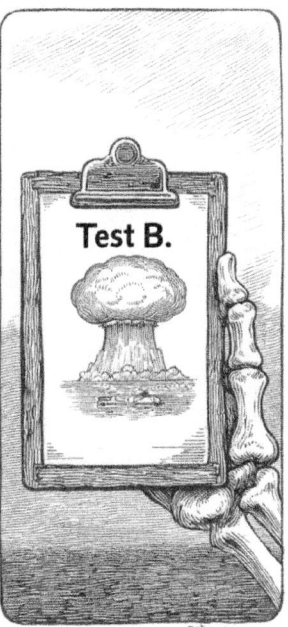

Nuclear weapons are the ultimate paradox: humanity's worst invention and yet its strangest insurance policy.

Nine's Company, Ten's a Crowd

Right now, nine countries definitely have nuclear weapons. The U.S. and Russia hold the bulk, like two kids hoarding all the fireworks at a party. Britain, France, and China joined early; India and Pakistan followed like squabbling neighbors who can't let the other get ahead. North Korea barged in late, shouting for attention, while Israel quietly pretends it just has a suspiciously glowing basement.

A few countries actually inherited nukes when the Soviet Union collapsed, Ukraine, Belarus, Kazakhstan, but they gave them up in the 1990s, trusting international promises. Ukraine alone traded away about 1,900 warheads, the third-largest stockpile in the world at the time, in exchange for security guarantees under the so-called Budapest Memorandum. Looking back, it's a bit like selling your fire extinguisher because the neighbors promised never to set anything on fire. Unsurprisingly, Ukraine now regrets the deal, especially after Russia's 2014 and 2022 invasions, and the irony bites deeper today, as President Zelensky continues to ask for the very security guarantees his country thought it had secured three decades ago.

Belarus and Kazakhstan also disarmed, hoping integration into the global order would bring stability and investment.

For a brief moment in the 1990s, it looked like nuclear weapons could actually shrink in number rather than multiply. But trust is fragile currency.

To stop the club from expanding, there's the Nuclear Non-Proliferation Treaty, signed in 1968 at the height of Cold War anxiety. It was essentially the world's awkward group chat where five official nuclear powers agreed, "We'll keep ours, you promise not to make new ones." The idea was noble: discourage arms races and encourage eventual disarmament. But the absurdity is obvious, nuclear haves telling the have-nots to stay clean while they clutched their own arsenals like toddlers guarding candy.

In practice, it's been a mix of progress and hypocrisy. Some nations signed on enthusiastically, others refused outright, and a few, like India, Pakistan, and Israel, treated the treaty like an invite they'd never RSVP to. North Korea even signed and later stormed out, proving exit doors exist. Still, without it, the world might have dozens of nuclear states today instead of nine, so the treaty remains a flawed but strangely useful band-aid on humanity's most dangerous wound.

Iran: Schrödinger's Bomb

For decades, the world has asked: is Iran building a nuke, or just really into suspicious uranium-spinning machines (centrifuges)? In the early 2000s, intelligence reports screamed "yes." Then came the 2015 nuclear deal, where Iran agreed to pause enrichment in exchange for sanctions relief. The Trump administration tore that up in 2018, and Iran promptly started tinkering again, like a teenager whose parents just left the house. Today, it's unclear whether Iran wants the bomb or just the leverage of maybe having the bomb. Either way, the world watches nervously.

Why Hiroshima, Why Nagasaki?

The U.S. had built two bombs. Hiroshima was chosen as the first target because it was a major military hub, untouched by previous bombings, which meant the weapon's full power could be measured. Three days later, Nagasaki got hit partly because it was on the backup list, partly because weather blocked other cities, and partly because the U.S. wanted to test a different bomb design.

Instead, think of it as the deadliest A/B test in history. In business, an A/B test is when companies show one group version A of something (say, a blue button on a website) and another group version B (maybe a red button) to see which performs better. The U.S. effectively did this with human lives, Hiroshima as test A, Nagasaki as test B, a comparison so grim it makes modern marketing look like child's play.

Hiroshima was selected as a primary military target with a significant industrial base and was largely untouched by conventional raids. That made it an ideal "pristine" canvas to showcase the destructive force of the uranium-based Little Boy bomb. The lack of prior damage meant every shattered building and burned district could be clearly attributed to the atomic blast, providing U.S. planners with stark, unambiguous data on the weapon's destructive potential.

Nagasaki, by contrast, was more of an accident of circumstance. The second bomb, the plutonium-based Fat Man, was intended for the city of Kokura. On August 9, however, Kokura was blanketed by clouds and smoke from another raid. With fuel running low, the bomber diverted to its secondary target, Nagasaki. This grim twist of weather and logistics highlights the almost arbitrary nature of the second strike. Beyond chance, the U.S. also wanted to test a different bomb design, an implosion device rather than a uranium gun-type, so dropping it offered both scientific data and psychological pressure. Two distinct bombs, two devastated cities: a chilling demonstration that America not only had the technology, but could use it again and again if Japan did not surrender.

Einstein's Big No-Show

Albert Einstein's name is tied to nukes because he co-signed a famous 1939 letter warning Roosevelt that Nazi Germany might build one. But Einstein never joined the Manhattan Project. He was too old, too politically radical for U.S. security clearances, and his brand of theoretical physics wasn't much help when the job was about metallurgy, chemistry, and engineering.

In plain English: the project needed lab rats, not stargazers. His famous equation, $E = mc^2$, is often linked to the bomb, but in reality it only shows the principle that a tiny bit of mass can release enormous energy. It explained the possibility of nuclear power, but it didn't give anyone blueprints for a bomb, more like showing that fire exists without telling you how to build a lighter.

Boom Town USA

The actual Manhattan Project was less about lone geniuses scribbling equations and more about a massive industrial effort. At its peak, it employed 130,000 people, cost more than the entire auto industry of the time, and turned sleepy towns into secret cities. Oak Ridge, Tennessee, buzzed with uranium enrichment plants; Hanford, Washington, churned out plutonium; Los Alamos, New Mexico, was the brainy desert hideout where Robert Oppenheimer and company pieced it all together. It was the natural follow-on from Einstein's equation, proof that mass could become energy, but now applied on an industrial scale.

Enter Robert Oppenheimer, the physicist who would become the reluctant face of the project. When he witnessed the first successful test in July 1945, he reached for the words of the Bhagavad Gita: "Now I am become Death, the Destroyer of Worlds." In the end, it wasn't a eureka moment, it was the biggest, most terrifying group project in history.

The project itself ran on a massive scale. At its peak, it employed more than 130,000 people and cost roughly $2 billion in 1945 dollars, tens of billions today. This was an enormous slice of America's wartime resources, funneled into secrecy and steel. And the secrecy was extraordinary, most workers at Oak Ridge or Hanford never knew they were building a bomb at all. Some thought they were working on a giant drying factory or even a super-refrigerator.

The climax came with the Trinity Test on July 16, 1945. A plutonium device nicknamed "the Gadget" was hoisted atop a 100-foot tower in the New Mexico desert. The explosion created a blinding flash, a shockwave felt 160 miles away, and a crater of green glass, trinitite, still visible today.

Oppenheimer's famous quote drew on his knowledge of Sanskrit and the Bhagavad Gita. In that text, the god Vishnu reveals his overwhelming, universal form to Prince Arjuna. Oppenheimer's words captured not just awe but also his sense of being an instrument of fate, swept into a role he could neither refuse nor escape.

After the war, Oppenheimer became a critic of the hydrogen bomb and a voice for international control of nuclear weapons. His stance cost him dearly. In 1954, a security hearing stripped him of his clearance, tarnishing the "father of the atomic bomb" as a man distrusted by the very government he had served. It is a tragic coda to a life spent at the intersection of genius, morality, and fear.

Hitler's Broken Science

How close did Nazi Germany actually get to the bomb? Not very. The Allies feared the worst, but German nuclear research was scattered, underfunded, and plagued by rivalries. Add in Hitler's obsession with "Aryan science" and dismissal of Jewish physicists, and the regime essentially kicked out many of the very minds, like Einstein, Szilárd, and Teller, who might have given them a chance. German physicist Werner Heisenberg dabbled with a reactor design, but it was small potatoes compared to the sprawling U.S. effort. In hindsight, America may have overestimated the Nazi threat, but in the shadow of World War II, "better safe than sorry" meant building the bomb first, just in case.

Chernobyl: The Reactor That Became a Ghost

If nukes show the destructive force of weapons, Chernobyl shows what happens when civilian nuclear power goes catastrophically wrong. On April 26, 1986, Reactor No. 4 at the Chernobyl Nuclear Power Plant in Soviet Ukraine exploded during a botched safety test.

The blast ripped through the reactor, releasing radioactive plumes that spread across Europe. Entire towns were evacuated, and a 19-mile exclusion zone still surrounds the site today, where wildlife now roams freely through the decaying remains of human habitation.

Gamers might know Chernobyl best from Call of Duty: Modern Warfare, where the eerie, abandoned city of Pripyat, complete with its rusting Ferris wheel, serves as the backdrop for one of the game's most iconic sniper missions. The haunting realism of that level came straight from the desolate landscape left behind by the disaster.

Radiation, the invisible killer, works by damaging living cells at the molecular level, breaking DNA and causing burns, sickness, and cancer. The science behind it is that unstable atoms shed energy in the form of particles or rays, alpha, beta, and gamma radiation. Alpha particles can be stopped by paper, beta by clothing or thin metal, but gamma rays can penetrate deep into the body, shredding cells as they go. That's why exposure is so dangerous: it's like being microwaved from the inside out.

First responders at Chernobyl experienced horrific acute radiation syndrome: vomiting, blistered skin, and in many cases, death within weeks. Some firemen reportedly reeked of metal before collapsing, a chilling sign of internal radiation damage. The long-term toll is still debated, but thousands of thyroid cancer cases have been linked to the fallout. Walking through Pripyat today feels like stepping into a time capsule of Soviet life abruptly frozen in 1986, an unsettling reminder that nuclear technology doesn't need a bomb to change the world forever.

Chapter 11

Edge of the World

Some places on Earth are so remote that getting pizza delivered would require a helicopter, a boat, and possibly divine intervention. These aren't just "off the beaten path" destinations, they're locations where the beaten path gave up, turned around, and went home to complain about the weather. From villages where cars run 24/7 to prevent freezing to ocean points where astronauts are your closest neighbors, these places prove that Earth still has locations where modern convenience goes to die.

Your Car Becomes a 24/7 Space Heater

Wake up in Oymyakon, Russia, and your morning routine begins with checking if your car survived the night. Residents leave their engines running continuously because turning them off is basically surrendering your vehicle to the arctic forever. Temperatures have hit -71.2°C, which is cold enough to freeze your breath before it leaves your mouth and turn boiling water into snow mid-air.

Your house looks like a fortress against the cold: thick log walls, tiny windows to minimize heat loss, and a roof so steep that snow slides off before it can accumulate into structural suicide. Indoor plumbing is a luxury that physics won't allow, pipes freeze solid, so most homes rely on outdoor toilets that become frozen monuments to human endurance. The local diet consists mainly of reindeer meat and frozen fish because growing vegetables in permafrost is like trying to garden on Mars.

The 500 residents have adapted to life where "warm" means anything above -40°C and where burying the dead requires lighting fires to thaw the permafrost. Schools only close when temperatures drop below -52°C, making every other place's snow day policies look embarrassingly soft. Your daily commute involves scraping ice off car windows that refreeze before you finish, and your heating bill would bankrupt a small country.

In Oymyakon, global warming isn't a political debate, it's a sincere personal wish. The town serves as a reminder that some places on Earth operate under their own rules, where basic survival requires abandoning every assumption about normal life, including the expectation that your bathroom should be inside your house.

The Loneliest Spot Has Space Neighbors

Point Nemo sits in the middle of the Pacific Ocean, so isolated from any land that astronauts on the International Space Station are literally closer to this spot than any human on Earth's surface when they orbit overhead at 408 kilometers altitude. Think about that for a second: there are people floating in space who are your nearest neighbors. This oceanic pole of inaccessibility is 2,688 kilometers from the nearest land in any direction, that's like being in London with your closest neighbor in Kiev.

It's where spacecraft go to die, NASA uses the area as a spacecraft cemetery because when you're decommissioning a 120-ton space station, you need somewhere it can crash without hitting anything important. The Mir space station ended up here in 2001, along with over 300 other pieces of space hardware. Mission control literally aims defunct satellites and stations at Point Nemo like cosmic darts, knowing that the worst-case scenario is disturbing some very lonely fish. The area has become humanity's designated "space junk goes here" zone, proving that even in the middle of absolute nowhere, we've found a way to turn it into a specialized dumping ground.

Arctic Town Runs on Helicopter Deliveries

Ittoqqortoormiit, Greenland, population 345, exists in a world where overnight shipping means "maybe next month if the weather cooperates." Getting there requires either a helicopter ride or a boat trip that's only possible during the brief summer months when the sea ice retreats enough to allow passage. For most of the year, the town is completely cut off from the outside world, surrounded by sea ice thicker than most people's driveways.

Residents hunt polar bears, seals, and arctic foxes for survival, while groceries arrive by helicopter at prices that would make airport food seem reasonable. A gallon of milk costs around $15, assuming the helicopter can land through the weather. The town has one school, one clinic, and exactly zero dating apps because everyone already knows everyone else's relationship history, career prospects, and how they handle their liquor.

Moving away requires space mission-level planning, weather windows, helicopter availability, and ice conditions must all align. Breakups get awkward when your ex lives in one of only 120 houses and leaving requires meteorological cooperation.

Tibetan Plateau Creates Its Own Weather

The Tibetan Plateau is so massive and high that it generates its own weather systems, earning the nickname "Roof of the World", though unlike most roofs, this one actively tries to kill you. At an average elevation of 4,500 meters, the air contains 40% less oxygen than sea level, forcing newcomers to spend days gasping like fish out of water while their bodies desperately recalibrate for survival.

The plateau spans 2.5 million square kilometers, larger than Western Europe, and sits so high that its sheer mass deflects jet streams and creates monsoon patterns across Asia. Weather systems literally bounce off it like a geographic pinball bumper, redirecting moisture and wind currents that determine rainfall from India to China. What happens on the plateau doesn't stay on the plateau; it reshapes climate for billions of people.

Altitude sickness here ranges from mild headaches to full hallucinations, with some visitors seeing things that aren't there while their oxygen-starved brains struggle to process reality. Acute mountain sickness can progress to cerebral edema, where your brain swells inside your skull until simple tasks become impossible. The human body, evolved for sea-level living, treats this elevation like a hostile alien environment, which, from a biological perspective, it essentially is.

Family Missed Fifty Years of History

In 1978, Soviet geologists exploring remote Siberian taiga discovered the Lykov family living in a primitive log cabin, completely unaware that World War II had happened, humans had reached the Moon, or that the outside world had changed at all. These Russian Old Believers had fled religious persecution in 1936 and spent over 40 years in complete isolation, surviving on wild game and whatever they could grow in the forest.

During one brutal winter, they ate their leather shoes to survive when crops failed. When found, they spoke an archaic form of Russian that had been distorted by decades of isolation from any outside influence; the geologists who discovered them initially mistook their speech as a sign that they were mentally disabled. The family had created an accidental time capsule where the 20th century simply never arrived. Tragically, three of the children died from illnesses in 1981, likely due to a lack of immunity to modern germs, and their father, Karp, passed away in 1988, leaving only one daughter, Agafia, as the last survivor.

While the rest of humanity experienced two world wars, the Cold War, space exploration, and countless technological revolutions, the Lykovs were just trying to make it through another Siberian winter without starving. Their isolation was so complete that history itself became optional, the ultimate unsubscribe from world events.

Professional Hermit Perfected Off-Grid Living

For 27 years, Christopher Knight lived alone in the Maine woods without human contact, becoming the "North Pond Hermit" who survived by stealing supplies from nearby cabins. He maintained a meticulously organized camp with a tent, sleeping bag, and stolen provisions, all hidden so effectively that he evaded detection for nearly three decades while living within miles of civilization.

Knight spent his days reading, meditating, and listening to radio broadcasts from a world he'd chosen to abandon entirely. In his 27 years of solitude, he spoke to exactly one person, a hiker he encountered by chance, before being caught in 2013. When asked why he'd done it, he simply said he liked being alone.

Knight had taken the modern fantasy of going "off-grid" to its most extreme conclusion, proving that true escape isn't just about finding a remote location, it's about completely severing the threads that connect you to everyone else. He turned antisocial behavior into a survival art form, showing that with enough dedication, you can disappear without leaving the zip code.

Professional Hermit Perfected Off-Grid Living

For 27 years, Christopher Knight lived hidden in the Maine woods, stealing food and supplies from cabins while avoiding all human contact. Known as the "North Pond Hermit," he built a camouflaged camp so well concealed that he went undetected for nearly three decades despite living just miles from civilization.

Knight spoke to only one person in all that time, a startled hiker, before being caught in 2013 and ending one of the longest known voluntary disappearances in modern history.

Chapter 12

Poisonous Delicacies

Food should be simple. If it tastes good and doesn't kill you, you're winning. But humans have spent centuries perfecting the art of making meals that blur the line between dinner and danger. These aren't accidents but deliberately risky foods that entire cultures have embraced, creating cuisines where proper preparation is literally the difference between satisfaction and the morgue.

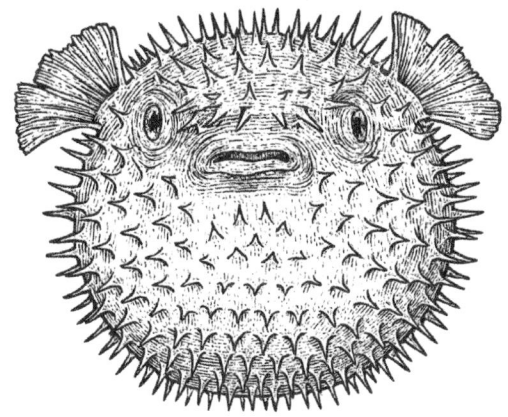

The pattern repeats across continents and cultures. Someone discovers that a potentially lethal ingredient tastes amazing if you prepare it just right, then entire societies decide this is worth the risk. It's as if humans looked at the natural world's "DO NOT EAT" warning labels and thought, "Challenge accepted."

Japan's Licensed-to-Kill Fish

Fugu contains enough tetrodotoxin to kill 30 adults, yet remains a prized delicacy that requires a government license to prepare. The poison concentrates in the liver, ovaries, and skin, making every slice a high-stakes decision where one wrong cut can transform dinner into a death sentence.

Chefs train for years to earn their fugu license, learning exactly where to place each incision to avoid puncturing the toxic organs. The certification process includes written exams, practical tests, and eating your own prepared fugu. It's the ultimate final exam where failure means more than a bad grade. Even licensed professionals occasionally get it wrong, with several deaths reported each year from both restaurant and home preparation.

The toxin causes paralysis while leaving victims fully conscious, and fugu restaurants charge premium prices despite the risks. It's culinary Russian roulette where the house always holds the loaded chamber.

The Fruit That Fights Back

Ackee looks innocent enough, but eating it before it naturally opens on the tree can cause "Jamaican vomiting sickness." This cheerfully named condition starts with nausea and can progress to hypoglycemic coma and death. The unripe fruit contains hypoglycin A, which prevents the body from properly metabolizing fats, essentially causing it to run out of fuel.

Jamaica has made ackee its national fruit despite these risks, pairing it with saltfish in a dish that requires careful timing and fruit selection. The fruit must be allowed to open naturally and turn bright red before dangerous toxins break down to safe levels. It's nature's way of teaching patience, since rushing to harvest can have consequences far beyond disappointment.

Anyone who's ever been tempted to eat fruit before it's properly ripe can understand the appeal. That perfect banana sitting on your counter isn't quite ready, but you're hungry now. With most fruit, the worst consequence is a slightly bitter taste. With ackee, impatience can put you in the hospital.

Italy's Underground Cheese Scene

Casu marzu exists in legal limbo, banned by EU food safety regulations but protected as traditional food in Sardinia. This cheese is deliberately infested with live insect larvae that digest the fats, creating a soft, pungent product that locals consider a delicacy. The maggots aren't just a side effect but essential to the cheese-making process.

The cheese is deliberately left exposed to flies in dark, humid environments where they lay their eggs. As the eggs hatch, the Piophila casei larvae begin digesting the fats, transforming the texture and flavor. Some Sardinians believe the cheese is only fit to eat when the maggots are still alive and active, viewing their movement as a sign of freshness.

The dining experience includes dodging flying larvae, since the maggots can jump several inches when disturbed. Some aficionados remove the maggots before eating, while others consume them as part of the authentic experience. There's something beautifully Italian about turning bureaucratic prohibition into cultural rebellion. The EU says you can't sell maggot cheese, so Sardinians make it anyway and call it heritage protection.

The Cyanide Staple

Cassava feeds over 800 million people worldwide, but contains compounds that release hydrogen cyanide when chewed raw. The distinction between life and death often comes down to knowing which variety you're dealing with. Sweet cassava has lower toxin levels and can often be eaten safely after just a quick boil, while bitter cassava contains high levels of cyanide and requires extensive, multi-step processing involving grating, soaking, and fermentation.

Traditional preparation methods developed over centuries ensure safety, but urbanization and changing food habits sometimes lead people to abandon these time-tested processes. During famines, the very people who most need nutrition are most likely to skip the safety steps that prevent poisoning. It's survival mathematics at its cruelest, where hunger and safety exist in constant tension.

The bitter irony cuts deep. A food that sustains hundreds of millions can be deadly if not prepared correctly. Cassava represents the knife-edge between sustenance and disaster in many developing regions, where proper knowledge and preparation techniques are literally matters of life and death. Mistaking one variety for another, or rushing the preparation process, can have fatal consequences that traditional wisdom was designed to prevent.

When Your Food Fights Back

San-nakji takes the concept of fresh food to its logical extreme. Live octopus is chopped into still-wriggling pieces that continue moving for several minutes after cutting. The tentacle segments can stick to your tongue, teeth, or throat during swallowing, and their suction cups create a genuine choking hazard. Several diners die each year from suffocation when pieces lodge in their airways.

The dish is typically served with sesame oil and a touch of salt. The oil helps reduce the suction power of the tentacles and makes them easier to swallow, while the salt enhances the flavor. The fact that an entire technique has been developed to mitigate the very risk that defines the dish adds a layer of cultural wisdom to the danger.

The appeal lies not just in freshness but in the sensation of active pieces moving in your mouth. It's perhaps the only food that literally tries to prevent you from eating it, turning dinner into a minor combat situation where both diner and dish are fighting for survival. There's something almost sporting about eating food that fights back, reminding us that eating was once a more primal activity where dinner didn't always cooperate with being consumed.

Hepatitis Lottery

Blood clams get their name from their red hemoglobin-rich liquid, but they're notorious for carrying waterborne diseases including hepatitis A, typhoid, and dysentery. These bivalves filter and concentrate pathogens from the contaminated waters where they're harvested, turning each clam into a potential disease vector.

The 1988 Shanghai hepatitis A epidemic stands as one of the largest foodborne outbreaks in history, with over 300,000 cases attributed to consuming uncooked or undercooked blood clams. The incident was so severe that it led to the city's blanket ban on blood clam sales, which remains a landmark example of how traditional delicacies can pose significant public health threats when modern sanitation is ignored.

Despite documented health risks, blood clams remain popular in parts of China where they're considered aphrodisiacs and prized for their unique metallic flavor.

The cooking process is often minimal since overcooking is said to ruin the texture and taste. It's Russian roulette with shellfish, where each bite carries the possibility of weeks in the hospital.

The economics of dangerous food create their own logic. If something is risky enough to be banned, it becomes more valuable to those willing to take the chance. Prohibition doesn't eliminate demand but drives it underground, where safety standards become even more questionable.

The Spice Rack's Hidden Danger

Nutmeg seems harmless enough in your kitchen cabinet, but consuming large amounts can cause hallucinations, seizures, and potentially death. The compound myristicin requires doses far beyond normal culinary use, typically several tablespoons, making accidental poisoning unlikely but intentional misuse dangerous. Historically, nutmeg was so valuable it triggered European colonial wars, with the Dutch trading Manhattan to the British in exchange for a nutmeg-producing island.

Modern cases usually involve teenagers experimenting with household substances, unaware that the dosage required for psychoactive effects is dangerously close to toxic levels. It's oddly comforting that even our spice racks harbor potential dangers, proving that humans will find a way to misuse almost anything if they're determined enough, even something as mundane as holiday baking spice.

Chapter 13

The Only Sure Thing Besides Death

"Nothing is certain except death and taxes,"

Benjamin Franklin observed in 1789, blissfully unaware that he'd just handed history's most creative bureaucrats a challenge. If taxes were inevitable, governments reasoned, why not make them memorable? What followed was two millennia of fiscal ingenuity that transformed everything

from bodily functions to facial hair into revenue opportunities.

The ancient world established the template: find something people do, use, or enjoy, then charge them for it. Romans perfected this art by taxing urine, proving that no human activity was too personal for governmental attention. Their successors took notes, expanding the concept to cover light, leisure, grooming habits, and eventually the very act of waste disposal. These six tales of taxation creativity reveal a consistent truth about power and money, when governments need cash, human dignity becomes negotiable, and bureaucratic imagination knows absolutely no bounds.

Liquid Gold

Urine had genuine market value in Ancient Rome thanks to its ammonia content. Laundries, or fullonicae, prized it as a natural detergent, soaking togas in the stuff to whiten and freshen the wool. Tanneries bought it to soften hides and strip away hair from animal skins. Even personal care made use of it: some Romans rinsed their mouths with urine for whiter teeth, while others applied it to skin as part of beauty routines. By modern standards it sounds horrifying, but at the time it was as normal as buying soap.

The Roman historian Suetonius tells us that Vespasian's son Titus objected to taxing such a foul product. The emperor simply held a gold coin to his son's nose and asked whether it smelled. When Titus admitted it did not, his father replied, "Yet it comes from urine." The phrase pecunia non olet, money does not stink, entered the

Roman vocabulary and still gets quoted today whenever politicians need to justify questionable revenue sources. Vespasian used the proceeds to help refill the empire's coffers after civil war, even funding the early construction of the Colosseum. His name remains linked to public urinals in France and Italy, where vespasiennes or vespasiani still stand as monuments to his very practical brand of taxation. Apparently, immortality comes in many forms, some emperors get statues, others get toilets.

Beard Tax Tokens

Vespasian's approach to unconventional taxation would inspire centuries of governmental creativity. In 1698, Tsar Peter the Great introduced a beard tax as part of his sweeping plan to modernise Russia along Western European lines. Beards, in his eyes, were symbols of the old, superstitious Russia he wanted to leave behind. Men who wanted to keep theirs had to pay an annual fee, scaled by social class, and carry a copper or silver token stamped with a bearded face and the words "money paid."

Refusal could result in a public shave administered by the Tsar's agents, who roamed the streets with scissors and razors. The policy infuriated traditionalists, especially Orthodox Christians who saw shaving as sinful, believing that God made man in His image, whiskers and all. Nobles paid 100 rubles annually, merchants 60, and even peasants entering cities faced a kopeck charge. The tokens became coveted collector's items, tiny bronze certificates of rebellion against royal grooming standards. Peter's beard tax proved that taxes can be more than financial, they can be tools of cultural revolution, turning facial hair into the ultimate political statement. Nothing says "modernization" quite like government-issued receipts for keeping your whiskers.

Daylight Robbery

If Russians thought facial hair taxation was excessive, Britain decided to go after light itself. The window tax of 1696 initially seemed like a fair property tax, charging homeowners based on the number of windows in their buildings. Houses with fewer than 10 windows paid a flat rate, but each additional opening cost extra. The logic seemed sound: bigger houses meant more windows, which meant wealthier owners who could afford higher taxes.

The reality was architectural vandalism on a national scale. Homeowners bricked up windows to avoid the charges, creating the distinctive blind windows still visible on Georgian terraces across Britain. New buildings were designed with minimal openings, prioritising tax avoidance over natural light. The phrase "daylight robbery" emerged from this period, when the government literally taxed illumination. Entire neighborhoods grew darker as families chose savings over sunlight. The wealthy could afford bright, airy homes, while the poor lived in deliberately gloomy boxes. After 156 years of bureaucratic blindness, the tax was finally repealed in 1851, but not before permanently scarring Britain's architectural landscape. The government had successfully managed to tax sunshine itself, a feat that would make modern energy companies weep with admiration.

Playing Card Duties

Britain's enthusiasm for taxing the seemingly untaxable extended beyond architecture to leisure activities. From 1712 to 1960, Britain imposed a stamp duty on playing cards that required the Ace of Spades to carry an official government stamp. This wasn't just about revenue, it was about preventing forgery and ensuring quality control in an era when playing cards were serious business. The penalties for producing unstamped cards included hefty fines and even transportation to the colonies.

The Ace of Spades became known as the "Death Card," not because of any mystical properties, but because it carried the government's official seal of approval. Card manufacturers like De La Rue built entire businesses around producing these elaborate, ornate stamps that turned a simple playing card into a miniature work of art. Smuggling unstamped cards became a cottage industry, with contraband decks hidden in everything from hollowed-out books to false-bottomed trunks.

The tax generated substantial revenue for nearly 250 years, proving that people will always find ways to gamble, even if the government takes a cut from every hand dealt. Britain had turned entertainment into a revenue stream, a lesson modern government would remember when they discovered video games and streaming services.

Hat Attack

While Britain perfected the art of taxing everyday objects, their colonial subjects across the Atlantic discovered that even clothing accessories weren't safe from bureaucratic overreach. The Hat Act of 1732 technically wasn't a tax but a trade restriction that banned American colonists from exporting hats to other colonies or countries, protecting British hat-makers from colonial competition.

The law was so specific it belonged in a comedy sketch: colonial hatters couldn't take on more than two apprentices at a time, apprenticeships had to last exactly seven years, and finished hats couldn't cross colonial borders.

The restrictions were nearly impossible to enforce across a continent, but they represented everything colonists hated about British rule: micromanagement of daily life for the benefit of merchants 3,000 miles away. American hatters ignored the law wholesale, creating a thriving underground millinery trade that foreshadowed larger rebellions to come. Smuggled beaver pelts crossed colonial boundaries hidden in grain shipments, while finished hats traveled disguised as everything from household goods to religious artifacts. The Hat Act became a rallying cry for colonial independence movements, proving that sometimes the smallest restrictions can trigger the biggest revolutions. Who knew that millinery could be so politically explosive?

Flush Fund

This tradition of governmental ingenuity survived well into modern times, proving that democracy hasn't diminished bureaucratic creativity one bit. The Chesapeake Bay Restoration Fee sounds respectable enough in official documents, but everyone calls it the flush tax, and for good reason. This flat annual charge appears on water bills like an unwelcome houseguest, demanding around $60 from anyone connected to public sewers or nursing a septic tank.

Unlike Vespasian's coin-sniffing approach, Maryland's version operates on elegant simplicity. Flush once a day or fifty times, the fee stays the same. The state cares nothing for your bathroom habits, only that you contribute to cleaning up the Chesapeake Bay's centuries of accumulated mess. Nitrogen and phosphorus have been choking the bay's famous blue crabs and oysters, turning one of America's most productive estuaries into an environmental disaster zone that stretches across six states.

The money flows straight into unglamorous but essential work: upgrading treatment plants, retrofitting septic systems, and preventing suburban lawns from bleeding fertiliser into waterways.

Critics initially balked at paying for something they considered a basic government service, but the results speak louder than complaints. Water clarity has improved measurably in several tributaries, and oyster populations show tentative signs of recovery.

Cow-Fart Tax

Modern governments continue pushing the boundaries of taxable activities, though not all experiments survive public scrutiny. In 2003, New Zealand proposed a "fart tax" on livestock, a levy on farmers for the methane gas emitted by their cows and sheep. This wasn't bureaucratic comedy, it was serious climate policy. Methane is a potent greenhouse gas, and New Zealand's millions of grazing animals contribute significantly to the country's carbon footprint.

The tax aimed to help meet international climate goals by making farmers accountable for their animals' atmospheric contributions. Farmers responded with predictable outrage, arguing that taxing biological functions would cripple their industry through bureaucratic absurdity.

The proposal faced international mockery and domestic political pressure before being quietly abandoned. It proved that some ideas, no matter how scientifically sound, are simply too ridiculous to survive contact with reality. Even governments have limits when it comes to monetising the natural world.

After two millennia of creative taxation, the taxman's imagination truly knows no bounds, well, almost no bounds.

Chapter 14

Death in Bulk

"Don't put all your eggs in one basket"

Sounds like timeless wisdom, but it's actually pandemic advice. The Black Death gave us quarantine (from the Italian quaranta giorni), taught us to avoid someone "like the plague," and coined the phrase "beyond the pale" when authorities literally marked infected areas with stakes and boundaries. Seven centuries later, we still "give someone a wide berth" and worry about things "spreading like

wildfire", linguistic souvenirs from humanity's first encounter with global biological catastrophe.

The plague killed a third of Europe between 1347-1351, but its real legacy isn't the death toll, it's how it accidentally invented modern life. Public health measures, labor markets, even our obsession with hygiene all trace back to a medieval world trying not to die horribly. Here's how a bacterial infection rewrote civilization, one panic-driven policy at a time.

Please Hold for 40 Days (No WiFi)

Venice invented the world's first isolation protocol, and it was basically medieval airplane mode that lasted over a month.

You've sailed for weeks to deliver silk and spices, only to anchor offshore while officials decide if you're carrying death along with your cargo. No Amazon Prime, no DoorDash, just you, your crew, and whatever hardtack you packed, floating in the Adriatic like a very expensive timeout. The Venetians called it quarantena (forty days), picking that number partly from the Bible and partly because thirty days wasn't cutting it for weeding out plague carriers. They built entire island hospitals called lazzaretti to house suspicious passengers while fumigating their goods with vinegar and smoke. Letters got holes poked through them, cloth bales were aired out, and spice jars were opened to the salt breeze.

But Venice didn't just wing it, they created the world's first public health board, the Provveditori alla Sanità

(Proveditors of Health), in 1486. This group of officials had the power to enforce quarantines, inspect ships and goods, and even close down sections of the city, essentially inventing bureaucratic pandemic response centuries before anyone knew what viruses were. The Lazzaretto Vecchio wasn't just a hospital but a complete isolation complex with separate areas for the sick, the suspected ill, and contaminated cargo, like a medieval CDC facility built on an island where nobody could escape the paperwork.

The system even produced its own iconic uniform: the plague doctor with his distinctive leather beak mask filled with strong-smelling herbs like mint and cloves. Based on miasma theory, the belief that disease spread through foul air, these doctors looked like nightmare birds stalking through quarantined areas, their beaks essentially medieval air purifiers that did absolutely nothing to prevent infection. It was like trying to debug your phone by taking it apart with medieval tools, but it sort of worked through sheer paranoid thoroughness.

Holy Hygiene Heresy

Medieval Europe believed disease was divine punishment, so washing your hands was basically giving God the finger. If sickness came from sin, then preventing it through earthly measures like cleanliness was borderline heretical.

The dominant medical theory focused on balancing your internal humours, blood, phlegm, yellow bile, and black bile, rather than scrubbing your fingernails. Most people figured that if God wanted you dead, soap wasn't going to save you. The miasma theory held that "bad air" entered through your pores, making excessive bathing dangerous because it opened your skin to disease. A protective layer of dirt was literally considered a medical defense mechanism, which explains why medieval people treated baths like medical procedures rather than daily maintenance.

Then the plague arrived and killed everyone with the impartiality of a malfunctioning algorithm. Priests died alongside prostitutes, saints alongside sinners, leaving survivors to wonder why their piety meant nothing to a bacterium. The Flagellants, who publicly whipped themselves to atone for collective sins, were decimated just as thoroughly as everyone else, further undermining the idea that spiritual purity offered any protection whatsoever.

The sheer randomness of who lived and died forced a radical rethink: maybe disease wasn't about moral failings, maybe it was just about germs that didn't give a damn about your confession schedule. Cities like Milan and Florence, desperate and running out of religious explanations, tried something revolutionary: practical solutions. They sealed infected houses, burned contaminated clothes, and created the first sanitation crews to haul away corpses and street waste. These weren't acts of faith, they were acts of pure terror-driven pragmatism. The obsession with hygiene we take for granted today started here, when medieval Europe realized that sometimes the most spiritual thing you can do is wash your bloody hands.

When Half Your Coworkers Ghosted (Permanently)

The Black Death accidentally invented capitalism's worst nightmare: a job market where workers had actual leverage, and feudal lords lost their minds faster than a startup CEO discovering unions.

With a third of Europe dead, suddenly everyone left standing could negotiate like they had multiple LinkedIn offers. Peasants started shopping around for better gigs, demanding actual wages instead of just feudal obligations, and lords had to compete for labor like tech companies fighting over developers. This created what economists would now call "demand-pull inflation" for labor, wages shot up while the price of goods skyrocketed due to the lack of workers to produce them.

Governments panicked and tried to cap wages at pre-plague levels, imagine if politicians tried to rollback salaries because too many people quit during the pandemic. The 1351 Statute of Labourers essentially made it illegal to ask for a raise or switch jobs, but reality doesn't care about laws when there's nobody left to harvest the crops. Workers changed villages under cover of darkness, negotiated perks like meals and shoes, and sometimes straight-up revolted. The oppressive law directly caused the Peasants' Revolt of 1381, proving that economic desperation plus legal stupidity equals political upheaval.

If you've ever leveraged a job offer to get a promotion, you're using a playbook written by medieval plague survivors who figured out that scarcity equals power. The Black Death didn't just give workers bargaining power, it was a key factor in ending feudalism entirely, as serfs gained enough leverage to abandon their lords' lands and fundamentally reshape the relationship between landowners and laborers forever.

The Chicken Cure (Spoiler: It Didn't Work)

Medieval doctors had a treatment for plague buboes that makes essential oils look like cutting-edge medicine: the Vicary Method, which involved strapping live chickens to your infected lymph nodes.

Named after English surgeon Thomas Vicary, this formalized technique required shaving a chicken's rear end and pressing its bare bottom against the swollen, agonizing bubo, hoping the bird would somehow "suck out" the poison like a feathered vacuum cleaner. When one chicken got tired (or died from the stress of being taped to a plague victim), they'd wash it, give it a break, then rotate in a fresh bird for the next shift. Some patients had multiple chickens working in relay, creating what was essentially a poultry ICU where the treatment was probably more traumatic than the disease.

The desperate creativity didn't stop with chickens. Wealthy patients consumed crushed emeralds mixed with food, while others rubbed dead snakes or pigeons on their buboes, creating a marketplace of expensive desperation where hope outweighed logic by astronomical margins. The logic was medieval humoural theory meets barnyard desperation, the chicken was believed to draw poison through its body, and when it died, doctors declared the "cure" was working. It's the medical equivalent of trying to fix your WiFi by taping a hamster to the router, except the hamster costs money and you're dying while it happens.

Death Influencers Started a Trend

The plague turned skull imagery into the medieval equivalent of going viral.

When funeral bells rang constantly and everyone was one sneeze away from the grave, memento mori became the hottest aesthetic. Artists painted Danse Macabre murals on church and cemetery walls across Europe, showing elaborate processions of skeletons and living people arranged by social rank, from pope and emperor to peasant and child, all dancing together toward their graves. These weren't just pretty pictures; they were powerful social commentary suggesting that death was the ultimate equalizer in a rigidly hierarchical society.

Churches commissioned chalky skeletons tugging rich people by the sleeve with captions basically saying "your money won't save you", the medieval version of "death comes for everyone" Instagram posts. Jewelers sold skull rings and bone-white prayer beads like designer accessories, while the obsession with mortality evolved into the Vanitas art movement, using symbols like hourglasses, skulls, and rotting fruit to remind viewers that earthly pleasures were ultimately meaningless.

The message was part existential dread, part life advice: remember you're going to die, so maybe stop being awful and get your affairs in order. It was doom-scrolling before screens existed, and somehow it helped people cope with living through humanity's worst biological nightmare by making death fashionable rather than just terrifying.

The Price of a Soul Soared

The plague didn't just change the labor market; it also created a spiritual inflation crisis. With so many priests dead, the wealthy faced a terrifying shortage of the very people they believed could save their souls from purgatory.

Memorial masses, prayers said after death to speed the journey to heaven, suddenly commanded premium prices as surviving clergy could charge whatever they wanted for afterlife services. This led to a boom in chantries, small chapels where families paid priests to pray for specific souls for eternity. The Black Death essentially created a spiritual real estate market where the rich desperately tried to buy guaranteed spots in heaven, proving that even death couldn't stop capitalism from finding new revenue streams.

Books Became Battlefield Casualties

The plague decimated the clergy who spent their lives hand-copying manuscripts in monastery scriptoriums. This created a massive shortage of books and a corresponding knowledge gap that would reshape how information spread through society.

With fewer monks available to painstakingly copy texts by hand, the old system of knowledge preservation collapsed almost overnight. The plague's disruption of manuscript production helped make the case for mechanical solutions to information reproduction. A century later, Gutenberg's printing press would revolutionize literacy and learning, partly because the Black Death had demonstrated just how fragile hand-copied knowledge could be when the people doing the copying started dying en masse.

The End of Feudal Architecture

The Black Death accelerated the decline of the medieval castle by making it impossible to maintain these massive stone monuments to feudal power. With the peasant population devastated and survivors demanding actual wages instead of unpaid labor, lords could no longer find the workforce needed to defend and maintain their fortresses.

The new, empowered peasant class refused to do free castle maintenance, forcing landowners to switch from feudal obligations to cash rents they often couldn't afford.

Many castles were abandoned or left to crumble, their decline serving as physical monuments to the feudal system's slow death. The plague helped usher in an era of more open, defensible manor houses, marking a clear architectural shift from the enclosed, militaristic world of the Middle Ages to something resembling modern land ownership.

Rat Smugglers Made It Worse

The Black Death's spread across Europe wasn't just bad luck, it was powered by logistics. Genoese merchant ships brought Yersinia pestis from the Crimean port of Kaffa in 1347, carrying black rats packed into grain stores like hidden biological grenades. Fleas living on those rats transmitted the bacteria, jumping hosts when their rodent meals died, and turning crowded ports into disease accelerators.

Attempts to stop the plague often backfired. Port cities banned visibly sick people but waved through their cargo, unaware that rats and fleas could carry death ashore unnoticed. Grain tariffs meant ships hoarded food, giving rats ideal floating habitats. Some cities even hired "rat catchers" who, not knowing rats spread plague, dumped captured rodents alive into rivers, letting them swim away and seed fresh outbreaks downstream. Medieval trade created the first global supply chain of death, proving that shipping efficiency and epidemiology are a catastrophic mix when your cargo squeaks.

Chapter 15

Border Chaos

Humans love drawing lines on maps, but reality doesn't always cooperate with our geometric fantasies. The difference between European and African borders tells the entire story of how boundaries get created.

Europe's borders evolved over centuries through wars, marriages, languages, and cultural divisions, creating squiggly lines that roughly follow rivers, mountains, and ethnic groups.

Africa's borders, by contrast, were drawn by European colonial administrators using rulers and complete ignorance of local geography, languages, or tribal territories.

The result is that European countries have borders that make some geographical and cultural sense, while African nations are often geometric shapes that slice through ethnic groups, split river systems, and create countries with dozens of different languages and cultures forced together by colonial convenience. These aren't just quirky tourist attractions, they're places where centuries-old treaty negotiations, colonial ambitions, and bureaucratic stubbornness created borders so complicated that GPS systems probably have nervous breakdowns trying to figure out which country you're standing in.

Belgium and Netherlands Play Geographic Jenga

Baarle is a town where the border between Belgium and the Netherlands looks like it was drawn by someone having a seizure while playing Tetris. The boundary zigzags through streets, shops, and individual houses, creating 22 Belgian exclaves within the Netherlands, some of which contain even smaller Dutch enclaves inside them. It's cartography's answer to Russian nesting dolls, except with more paperwork.

Residents regularly cross international borders just walking to their kitchen. Some houses have front doors in the Netherlands and back doors in Belgium, while others are split down the middle with different tax rates applying to each half. GPS systems here get so confused that they just start suggesting "take the next turn… into a different country!" and give up on directions entirely. During COVID-19 lockdowns, the Belgian side of cafes had to close while the Dutch side remained open, creating the world's most geographically specific drinking restrictions.

House numbers determine nationality, if your front door number corresponds to a Belgian address, you're Belgian, even if most of your house sits in the Netherlands. This creates practical complications: Belgian residents pay higher income taxes but enjoy more generous social benefits, while Dutch residents face lower tax rates but different healthcare systems. A house split between countries might have the kitchen taxed at Belgian rates while the living room falls under Dutch jurisdiction.

Property taxes, business licenses, and even which emergency services respond depend entirely on which side of the invisible line you're standing on. Shops routinely operate under two different tax systems simultaneously, with separate cash registers for each nationality's customers. During the EU's early years, currency exchanges happened mid-transaction as customers moved between the Belgian franc and Dutch guilder sections of the same store.

The World's Only Unclaimed Land

Bir Tawil sits in the desert between Egypt and Sudan as the only piece of land on Earth that no country wants to claim. Both nations refuse to acknowledge sovereignty over this 2,060-square-kilometer patch of sand and rock, creating a legal vacuum that exists because neither side wants to give up their claim to the much larger and more valuable Halaib Triangle nearby.

The bizarre standoff stems from colonial-era border disputes where two different treaties drew two different boundaries. Egypt prefers the 1899 line that gives them the Halaib Triangle but not Bir Tawil, while Sudan prefers the 1902 line that reverses the situation. Since claiming Bir Tawil would legally undermine their respective claims to Halaib, both countries actively reject sovereignty over what might be the world's least desirable real estate.

Navigation apps in Bir Tawil don't even try to give directions; they just display a single error message and quit. This has made the territory a magnet for aspiring micronation founders who dream of planting flags and declaring independence in humanity's only truly available territory, though their "kingdoms" remain monuments to bureaucratic stubbornness rather than actual governance.

Library Where Crossing Borders Is Required Reading

The Haskell Free Library and Opera House straddles the US-Canada border so precisely that you literally cannot use the building without committing an international border crossing. The entrance sits in Derby Line, Vermont, but the book collection and opera stage are located in Stanstead, Quebec, creating the only library in the world where checking out books requires crossing national boundaries.

A black line painted on the floor marks where Vermont ends and Quebec begins, running directly through the reading room and across the stage. Patrons enter through US customs, walk past American magazines, then cross into Canada to browse the main collection. During heightened border security periods, librarians needed special permits to move books between countries, while opera performers required passports to walk from dressing rooms to the stage. Tourists' phones constantly flicker between American and Canadian mobile carriers, turning every step into a data-roaming international incident.

Germany's 450-Kilometer Geography Mistake

Namibia's Caprivi Strip exists because German colonial negotiators in 1890 were convinced they needed river access to the Indian Ocean, creating a 450-kilometer-long panhandle that looks like someone attached a geographical tail to the country. This narrow corridor, barely 32 kilometers wide at its narrowest point, stretches across southern Africa like a geographic anomaly that separates Botswana from Angola and Zambia.

The Strip was designed to give German South West Africa access to the Zambezi River and theoretically provide a route to German East Africa, though the Victoria Falls made this waterway considerably less useful than Berlin had hoped. The result is a piece of Namibia that shares borders with four different countries while being almost entirely disconnected from the rest of Namibia by geography and culture.

Today, the Strip remains a logistical nightmare where traveling between its eastern and western ends requires crossing multiple international borders or making an enormous detour through Namibian territory. The German Empire is long gone, but its spirit lives on in every trucker who curses a colonial mapmaker while stuck in customs lines at the edge of the Strip. Despite being sliced into four countries, the one cultural constant is that everyone agrees the fishing is better on the other side of the border.

Vatican City's Invisible Border Control

Vatican City operates the world's most relaxed international border, a painted line on the ground that you can cross by taking a slightly longer step. At 0.17 square miles, it's the smallest sovereign nation on Earth, entirely enclosed within Rome and separated from Italy by barriers that range from medieval walls to simple white lines painted on cobblestones.

Most visitors accidentally commit multiple border crossings without realizing it. St. Peter's Square technically lies within Vatican territory, meaning tourists posing for photos are unknowingly standing in a foreign country while their friends snap pictures from Italy. The Vatican operates its own postal system, issues its own euros, and maintains separate laws within its borders, all while being physically indistinguishable from the surrounding Roman streets. It operates more like a very elaborate building with its own government than a traditional country with defensible borders.

Chapter 16

Writer's Block

Writer's block is that psychological dead zone where your creativity shuts down completely, you sit staring at blank pages, overwhelmed by either too many ideas or none at all. Paralyzed by perfectionism, stress, or the simple terror that nothing you write will be worth reading.

It manifests as inability to start, stagnation mid-project, or that familiar cycle of procrastination where cleaning your entire house suddenly seems more urgent than meeting your deadline.

The causes range from burnout and anxiety to self-doubt and disconnection from your work's purpose.

Most people facing creative paralysis try the usual remedies: taking breaks, changing environments, or forcing themselves to write terrible first drafts. But history's greatest authors took more extreme approaches, developing work habits that would get them fired from any normal job, banned from most coffee shops, and possibly committed for psychiatric evaluation. These weren't just quirky preferences; they were elaborate systems of creative self-torture that somehow produced literary masterpieces. The question becomes: what lengths would you go to in order to break through your creative barriers and get back to productive work?

Naked and Locked Away

When procrastination threatened to derail "Les Misérables," Victor Hugo created his own prison system. He gave his clothes to his servant and locked himself in his study wearing nothing but a blanket. The logic was simple: if he couldn't get dressed, he couldn't go outside and avoid writing. This method worked so well that he completed one of literature's longest novels while essentially under house arrest by his own clothing.

Hugo's servant held his wardrobe hostage until daily writing quotas were met, creating a system where literary productivity was literally measured in returned garments. The man who wrote about social justice and human dignity apparently needed to strip himself of basic dignity to write about it. His naked writing sessions produced over 1,400 pages of social commentary, proving that great art sometimes requires sacrificing personal comfort for creative necessity.

Rotten Apple Aromatherapy

Inside Friedrich Schiller's desk drawers lay an unusual creative tool: piles of rotting apples. He claimed the stench of fermenting fruit inspired his best work, and his wife reported that he couldn't write unless the smell of decay was wafting around his study. This turned his workspace into an olfactory nightmare that somehow produced beautiful poetry and groundbreaking drama.

This wasn't just eccentricity, Schiller genuinely believed that the smell of decomposition sparked his creativity, as if his brain needed to process decay before it could create beauty. Visitors to his home were often overwhelmed by the putrid smell emanating from his writing area, while Schiller sat contentedly composing works about human nobility and philosophical ideals. He literally surrounded himself with rot to write about beauty, demonstrating that inspiration can come from the most unlikely sources.

High-Octane Writing Fuel

Coffee fueled Honoré de Balzac's writing career in ways that would concern modern health professionals. He consumed 40-50 cups daily and sometimes ate coffee grounds straight from the bag, believing concentrated caffeine enhanced his writing abilities. His ritual began at 1 AM when he'd wake up and start writing until 8 AM, powered entirely by massive amounts of stimulation.

When regular coffee stopped providing sufficient energy, he switched to eating dry grounds, turning his digestive system into a processing plant for caffeine. Friends and doctors expressed concern that his intake was reaching problematic levels, but he insisted that coffee was essential to his creative process. He wrote prolifically, producing 85 novels and numerous short stories, though his intensive work schedule and stimulant use likely contributed to his death at 51.

Bathtub Murder Lab

Bath time became creative time for Agatha Christie, who plotted murders while soaking in hot water and eating apples. She claimed her best plot twists came to her while relaxing in the tub, turning what most people used for hygiene into a space where she'd work out alibis, motives, and methods for dozens of fictional murders.

Christie's bathroom became her creative headquarters where she'd spend hours submerged in water, mentally experimenting with poisons, weapons, and locked-room mysteries. Unlike Schiller's reliance on rotting fruit for inspiration, Christie preferred her apples fresh and crisp while brainstorming death, a peculiar irony that while her characters frequently drowned or were poisoned, she found inspiration while literally soaking in water and consuming the forbidden biblical fruit. Her apple-eating bath sessions produced over 80 detective novels and made her one of the best-selling authors in history.

The 120-Foot Manuscript

Paper changes interrupted Jack Kerouac's creative flow, so he solved the problem by eliminating paper changes entirely. He typed "On the Road" on a single 120-foot roll of paper, taping regular sheets together into one continuous scroll and feeding it through his typewriter. This created a manuscript that looked more like an ancient proclamation than a modern novel.

Kerouac was a restless spirit who'd spent years drifting across America, working railroad jobs, washing dishes, and absorbing the rhythms of a country in post-war transition. He'd hitchhiked thousands of miles, slept in bus stations, and lived with jazz musicians, collecting experiences that would eventually pour onto that famous scroll. The Beat Generation writer believed that spontaneous prose should mirror spontaneous living, interrupting the writing process with mechanical tasks like changing paper felt like betraying the natural flow of thought and memory.

Anyone who's ever been "in the zone" while working understands Kerouac's frustration with arbitrary interruptions. You know that feeling when you're finally hitting your stride on a project, ideas flowing freely, and then your computer crashes or someone needs you to find a stapler? That moment when external reality intrudes on internal momentum can completely derail creative progress. Kerouac's scroll was his way of building a bridge across that gap, creating a physical writing surface that could match the endurance of his mental energy.

The scroll method eliminated all interruptions, no pausing to load new paper, no breaking momentum to organize pages. Kerouac could follow his stream-of-consciousness style without any physical barriers, creating a writing process that matched his spontaneous prose style. When he finished after a three-week intensive session, he had a 120-foot manuscript that unrolled like a medieval scroll containing pure 1950s American rebellion. Publishers initially struggled with the format, how do you edit something that can't be separated into pages? But the scroll itself became part of the book's legend, a physical artifact that embodied the continuous journey it described.

Sterile Hotel Sanctuary

Hotel rooms became Maya Angelou's preferred writing studios, but not the way most people would use them. She rented rooms specifically for writing, then asked staff to strip them completely bare, no artwork, no decorations, no distractions. This created sterile writing environments where she could focus entirely on words, arriving with only a thesaurus, a Bible, and writing materials.

Angelou's method eliminated all visual stimulation that might interfere with her concentration, creating environments so minimal they resembled meditation spaces more than typical work areas. She'd work with a legal pad in these deliberately sparse, impersonal rooms because she believed that removing comfort and familiar surroundings helped her focus on the essential task of writing.

Chapter 17

Wild Outbreaks of Mass Hysteria

Mass hysteria, also called mass psychogenic illness, shows how powerful the mind can be when fear and stress ripple through a group.

Entire communities have collapsed into bizarre behaviours, convinced they were bewitched, poisoned, or under attack.

What follows are some of the strangest documented outbreaks across history, each one fuelled not by germs or toxins, but by the contagious spread of belief and emotion.

Dance Until You Drop

In the summer of 1518, Strasbourg became the stage for one of history's strangest spectacles.

At the time, Strasbourg was a bustling city in the Holy Roman Empire, but life for the average townsman was harsh. The people of Strasbourg were living under unimaginable stress. In the years leading up to 1518 the region endured successive famines and epidemics, including outbreaks of smallpox and syphilis. These disasters left households hungry, weakened, and deeply anxious. Grinding poverty pressed on peasants and artisans alike, while the narrow-cobbled streets, though noisy with markets and livestock, echoed with worry over crop failures, taxation, and the ever-present threat of disease. Life was brutal and desperate, creating a population primed for a psychological breakdown.

Against this backdrop of daily stress and fear, strange collective behaviors found fertile ground. Enter Frau Troffea, who stepped into the street and began dancing as though the cobblestones had turned into a medieval dance floor. She didn't stop after an hour, or even a day, it was less "let's have a jig" and more "try to out-dance death itself." By the end of the week, dozens had joined her, flailing and stomping like possessed partygoers until they collapsed in sheer exhaustion.

The events of 1518 were so extraordinary that they appear in city council notes, physician records, and local chronicles, leaving behind a paper trail of disbelief. These accounts insist that people didn't just dance until they dropped, they literally danced themselves to death.

One chronicler even stated that at the height of the epidemic as many as fifteen people were dying per day. The deaths were not blamed on any disease but on sheer physical exhaustion, strokes, heart attacks, or simply collapsing after days without food, water, or sleep.

Eyewitnesses described dancers with bruised and bloodied feet, still unable to stop their frantic movements.

Modern historian John Waller estimates that the total death toll may have reached around one hundred, based on these accounts and extrapolations. Meanwhile, city leaders, desperate for a solution, bizarrely believed more dancing would purge the sickness. They hired musicians and even built a stage, effectively turning mass hysteria into a deathly carnival. This misguided "cure" only fueled the frenzy, a vivid reminder of how fear and stress can twist communal logic into disaster.

But why did it happen? Some explanations have been offered, from ergot-poisoned bread to secret religious cults. Ergot poisoning makes sense on paper, it causes convulsions and hallucinations, but in reality, it usually leaves people writhing in pain, not waltzing in the streets for days. And while some scholars imagine heretical sects using ecstatic dancing as protest, contemporary witnesses were clear: these people weren't celebrating, they were suffering. The truth is messier, and probably lies in a cocktail of stress, hunger, faith, and fear that made whole communities snap in unison.

The Biting Nuns

In the cloistered world of a 15th-century German convent, repression and routine created a pressure cooker of emotions. One day, a nun began biting her fellow sisters. It sounds like mischief, but the behavior spread uncontrollably across convents, with nuns in the

Netherlands and even Italy succumbing to the compulsion.

Why biting? Historians believe it reflected pent-up frustrations in rigid, isolated communities where emotional expression was nearly forbidden. Religious authorities initially claimed demonic possession and attempted exorcisms, but when those rituals failed, they threatened harsh physical punishment. Fear of the lash achieved what prayer and ritual could not: the epidemic stopped.

Other outbreaks in convents were even stranger, some nuns were documented meowing in chorus for hours each day, turning the cloister into something closer to a barnyard opera than a house of prayer. Imagine the bewildered neighbors hearing a choir of cats echo from behind convent walls.

These surreal spectacles likely grew from the same brew of strict discipline, psychological pressure, and the suffocating lack of emotional outlet. In modern terms, this is social contagion, the idea that one person's odd behavior can spread through a group the way yawning does, except with more meowing. When feelings are bottled too tightly, they sometimes come out as claws and caterwauls instead of hymns, showing that moods and actions can be as infectious as colds.

Bewitched in Salem

In 1692, the Puritan town of Salem, Massachusetts, became consumed by fear of the devil. A small group of girls began to twitch, scream, and collapse in dramatic fits, claiming invisible spirits tormented them. The performances carried weight in a society primed to see Satan's hand in every misfortune.

Soon, accusations spread like wildfire, neighbors accusing neighbors, children accusing adults, even a four-year-old girl dragged into the madness. Over 200 people stood trial, often on flimsy "spectral evidence," meaning visions or dreams. Nineteen were hanged, one unfortunate dog was executed as a supposed witch, and Giles Corey, an 81-year-old farmer, was pressed to death under heavy stones for refusing to plead. His silent resistance meant his land could not be seized, protecting his family's inheritance.

What fuelled it? Beyond religious paranoia, Salem was a community strained by economic rivalries, recent war trauma, and a rigid belief in divine punishment. The girls' symptoms were real, but their meaning was twisted by a society eager for scapegoats, much like the convent nuns who turned repression into bites and meows, or the dancers of Strasbourg who stomped themselves into the grave. Different times, different stages, but the same script of stress erupting in strange, contagious ways.

Tanganyika, 1962

At a mission school in newly independent Tanganyika (now Tanzania), three girls erupted into uncontrollable laughter. Teachers assumed it would pass, but the giggles spread like fire through the dormitories, escalating into fits of laughter, tears, fainting, and anxiety. Within weeks, the school was forced to shut down, and the strange "epidemic" spread to nearby villages.

In total, more than 1,000 people were affected across 14 schools and communities, with some episodes lasting over a week. Psychologists point to the stress of independence and the crushing academic pressures placed on children in this transitional society. The outbreak demonstrated how social tension can manifest physically, especially in groups under strict control. Unlike viruses, hysteria spreads not through the air but through observation, seeing someone lose control can, ironically, make others do the same.

The June Bug Epidemic

In 1962, a U.S. textile mill in the South became the unlikely stage for a mystery. Whispers spread about a biting insect, the so-called "June bug", prowling the factory floor. Before long, dozens of workers complained of dizziness, nausea, vomiting, and fainting.

Production lines shut down, and investigators descended to hunt for the culprit. No insects turned up, and chemical tests revealed nothing. The outbreak was fueled not by pests, but by panic. In stifling, poorly ventilated conditions, ordinary aches and fatigue were reimagined as the work of a phantom bug. The rumor magnified each symptom until the factory resembled a ward of the stricken.

One explanation is the nocebo effect, the dark mirror of the placebo effect. Where a placebo makes people feel better simply because they expect to, a nocebo does the opposite: the expectation of illness produces real suffering. Workers convinced a bug was lurking began to feel bitten whether or not it existed, and nausea, rashes, and dizziness quickly followed.

Another layer was social contagion, the human tendency to "catch" behaviors and emotions from those around us. Just as yawns or laughter ripple through a room, fear can do the same, only this time dressed up as an insect invasion. Once a few collapsed, others soon followed.

Groupthink likely played its part too. In a tense, stressful environment, nobody wanted to be the lone sceptic while colleagues keeled over, so fainting and complaints spread shift by shift. Reports recorded near-synchronized bouts of illness despite the absence of any bug at all. The episode illustrates how expectation, imitation, and conformity combined to conjure a full-scale epidemic from nothing more than rumour.

Chapter 18

Fake It 'Til You Make It

"The public will believe anything, so long as it is not founded on truth."

Humans have an extraordinary capacity for believing absolute nonsense, especially when it's packaged with just enough authority to sound legitimate.

Throughout history, con artists, pranksters, and opportunists have exploited this weakness with hoaxes so outrageous that they should have been spotted from orbit. Yet these deceptions didn't just fool a few gullible individuals, they convinced entire societies, sparked scientific debates, launched careers, and in some cases changed the course of history.

The pattern repeats across centuries: someone presents fabricated evidence, adds a dash of scientific-sounding language, gets a few respected authorities to endorse it, and suddenly half the world believes in moon civilizations or mechanical chess wizards. The most successful hoaxes weren't just lies, they were masterclasses in understanding human psychology, revealing our desperate desire to believe in the extraordinary, our tendency to trust authority figures, and our reluctance to admit we've been fooled.

Bat People Living Large on the Moon

In August 1835, the *New York Sun* published the most successful newspaper hoax in history, claiming that British astronomer Sir John Herschel had discovered life on the Moon using a powerful new telescope. The reports, supposedly reprinted from the *Edinburgh Journal of Science*, described a lunar paradise populated by bat-winged humanoids, herds of bison-like creatures, and magnificent crystal temples that reflected sunlight like cosmic disco balls.

The articles were written with scientific precision that made them sound believable. They described the telescope's revolutionary capabilities in technical detail, explained the lunar creatures' anatomy with zoological authority, and even included observations about lunar geography that matched existing astronomical knowledge. Readers devoured every word, circulation of the *Sun* quadrupled overnight, and telescope sales across New York City boomed as curious citizens tried to spot the moon creatures themselves.

The hoax succeeded because it exploited the perfect storm of public fascination with astronomy, limited scientific communication, and the growing credibility of newspapers as information sources. In 1835, space was genuinely mysterious territory where almost anything seemed possible. The idea that the Moon might harbor life wasn't scientifically absurd, just unproven, which made the *Sun's* "discoveries" tantalizingly plausible.

What made the deception particularly brilliant was its gradual revelation strategy. The first article simply announced Herschel's new telescope. The second revealed basic lunar landscape details. Only in subsequent installments did the truly extraordinary claims emerge, by which point readers were already invested in the story. The hoax also leveraged Herschel's genuine reputation, he really was a respected astronomer, though he was actually in South Africa at the time and had no idea his name was being attached to fictional moon bats.

The truth emerged when other newspapers tried to contact the *Edinburgh Journal of Science* for more details, only to discover that the journal had ceased publication years earlier. The *Sun* eventually admitted the hoax but never apologized, claiming it had been intended as satire that got out of hand. The damage to public trust was minimal, partly because readers had enjoyed being fooled by such an entertaining story, and partly because the hoax had been so well-crafted that being deceived by it felt almost like a compliment to their imagination.

Yorkshire's Paper Fairy Ring

The Cottingley Fairies became the most famous photographic hoax of the early 20th century, proving that even primitive special effects could fool sophisticated adults when they desperately wanted to believe. In 1917, two young girls in Yorkshire, Elsie Wright and Frances Griffiths, produced photographs showing themselves playing with tiny winged fairies in their garden. The images looked exactly like what they were: paper cutouts held up with hatpins, but the fairy photographs captivated a public hungry for magic in the aftermath of World War I.

The hoax gained credibility when the girls' parents showed the photographs to Edward Gardner, a prominent member of the Theosophical Society, who declared them genuine evidence of fairy life. Gardner's endorsement attracted the attention of Sir Arthur Conan Doyle, creator of the ultra-rational Sherlock Holmes, who was ironically a passionate believer in spiritualism and the supernatural. Doyle wrote articles for *The Strand Magazine* presenting the photographs as proof that fairies existed, lending his considerable literary reputation to what were essentially children's art projects.

What made the Cottingley case particularly fascinating was how it revealed the collision between scientific skepticism and spiritual yearning in post-war Britain. The photographs were technically crude, the fairies were clearly two-dimensional, and their poses were suspiciously similar to illustrations from popular children's books. Yet respected adults, including photographic experts, declared them authentic because they fulfilled a psychological need to believe in wonder and magic during a period of massive social upheaval.

The girls maintained their story for decades, partly because they were children when it started and partly because admitting the hoax would have embarrassed prominent adults who had championed their cause. Frances and Elsie only confessed in the 1980s, explaining that they had cut the fairy figures from a popular children's book called *Princess Mary's Gift Book* and arranged them in the garden with hatpins and thread. They expressed amazement that anyone had believed the photographs, especially since the fairies were obviously flat and appeared to be dancing in mid-air without any visible means of support.

The Cottingley Fairies demonstrated how photographic evidence, which seemed objective and scientific, could be manipulated to support almost any claim. More importantly, it showed how the authority of respected endorsers could transform obvious fakes into accepted facts, a lesson that remains relevant in our current era of digital manipulation and viral misinformation.

The Chess-Playing Mechanical Turk

The Turk was perhaps history's most successful long-term hoax, a supposed chess-playing automaton that defeated aristocrats, intellectuals, and even Napoleon Bonaparte across Europe and America from 1770 to 1854. The machine appeared to be a mechanical marvel: a wooden figure dressed in Ottoman robes sitting behind a chess cabinet, capable of playing world-class chess without any apparent human intervention. What audiences saw was the birth of artificial intelligence. What they were actually watching was an elaborate magic trick powered by a full-sized human chess master hidden inside the cabinet.

The deception was engineered by Wolfgang von Kempelen, a Hungarian inventor who created the Turk to entertain Empress Maria Theresa of Austria. The cabinet was designed with a complex system of sliding panels, hidden compartments, and false doors that allowed a chess expert to conceal himself inside while operating the automaton's arms through an intricate system of levers and pulleys. Before each performance, Kempelen would open various cabinet doors to show the audience that the machine contained only clockwork gears and mechanical components, carefully avoiding the compartments where the human operator was hiding.

The Turk's chess games were genuine competitions played by skilled masters who could see the board through a magnetic system beneath the surface. The hidden player would move his own pieces on a duplicate board inside the cabinet, while the automaton's movements above were controlled through mechanical linkages. The operator had to remain cramped and silent for hours, sweating in the confined space while playing against some of Europe's finest chess minds. Between games, the human player would exit through a secret panel in the cabinet's back, but audiences never suspected that the machine's chess brilliance came from very human intelligence.

The hoax succeeded for over 80 years because it exploited the era's fascination with mechanical innovation while staying just ahead of technological possibility. In the 18th and 19th centuries, clockwork automatons were genuinely sophisticated, capable of writing, drawing, and playing musical instruments, so a chess-playing machine seemed like a natural extension of existing technology. The Turk's performances were also carefully managed to maintain the illusion: it occasionally made mistakes to seem more believable, sometimes required winding up like a clock, and periodically needed repairs that allowed operators to be secretly replaced.

The hoax finally ended when the machine was exposed after being purchased by a museum in Philadelphia. By then, the Turk had inspired serious discussions about artificial intelligence, influenced early computer science concepts, and demonstrated that audiences were willing to believe in mechanical thinking long before the technology actually existed. The deception revealed humanity's simultaneous fascination with and anxiety about the possibility of intelligent machines, themes that remain central to our relationship with technology today.

Scotland's Submarine Monster

The "Surgeon's Photograph" of 1934 became the most famous piece of evidence for the Loch Ness Monster, a grainy black-and-white image showing what appeared to be a long-necked creature rising from the dark waters of Scotland's most famous lake. The photograph was supposedly taken by Robert Kenneth Wilson, a respected London gynecologist, lending medical authority to what would become the poster image for cryptozoology and Scotland's tourism industry. For sixty years, the picture was analyzed, debated, and reproduced in countless books and documentaries as the best proof that an ancient creature survived in Loch Ness. The image showed exactly what people wanted to see: a serpentine neck emerging from the water, suggesting a creature large enough to match descriptions of the legendary monster but distant enough to maintain mystery. Photography was still considered objective evidence in 1934, and the idea that a medical doctor would fabricate such evidence seemed implausible to most observers.

The truth emerged in 1994 when Christian Spurling, the last surviving conspirator, confessed on his deathbed that the photograph showed a toy submarine with a sculpted head attached, floating in a shallow part of the loch. The hoax had been orchestrated by Marmaduke Wetherell, a hunter humiliated by earlier failed attempts to find the monster, who convinced Wilson to present the photograph as his own discovery. The "creature" was actually about two feet long, and the photograph was taken from a low angle to make it appear much larger and more distant. Even after the confession, many Nessie believers continued to argue that the photograph showed a real creature, illustrating how deeply held beliefs can survive contradictory evidence and how a single compelling image could sustain a myth for decades while generating substantial tourism revenue for Scotland.

Barnum's Grotesque Goldmine

P.T. Barnum's Fiji Mermaid represented American showmanship at its most audacious, a deliberate fake so obviously artificial that its success said more about audience psychology than the quality of the deception. In 1842, Barnum purchased what he claimed was the preserved body of a real mermaid, caught off the coast of Fiji and brought to America by a sea captain desperate for money. What visitors to Barnum's American Museum actually saw was the torso of a juvenile monkey stitched to the tail of a large fish, creating a grotesque hybrid that looked more like a nightmare than a mythical sea creature.

The exhibit was deliberately repulsive, with dried, leathery skin, bared teeth, and clawed hands that made viewers recoil rather than marvel. Barnum knew exactly what he was selling and never seriously claimed the creature was real, though his promotional materials were carefully worded to suggest authenticity without making claims that could be legally challenged. The mermaid was displayed alongside other curiosities, freaks, and oddities that made up Barnum's collection of the strange and unusual.

The success of the Fiji Mermaid revealed the entertainment value of being fooled, as long as the audience was in on the joke to some degree. Visitors paid their money knowing they might see something fake, but they were willing to suspend disbelief for the sake of spectacle. Barnum understood that people didn't necessarily want to see real mermaids, they wanted to experience the thrill of encountering something extraordinary, even if they suspected it was artificial.

Barnum marketed the exhibit with typical showman flair, creating elaborate backstories about the specimen's discovery and hiring actors to pose as scientists who would vouch for its authenticity. The promotional campaign was often more entertaining than the exhibit itself, demonstrating Barnum's genius for creating desire through storytelling rather than relying solely on the physical evidence. He famously declared that "there's a sucker born every minute," though he understood that his customers were often complicit in their own deception, choosing to believe in order to enhance their entertainment experience.

The Fiji Mermaid established the template for modern entertainment hoaxes, where the line between truth and fiction is deliberately blurred to create spectacular experiences. Barnum's approach influenced everything from carnival sideshows to reality television, proving that audiences would pay premium prices for carefully crafted illusions as long as they provided sufficient spectacle and storytelling.

The Hitler Diaries Disaster

The Hitler Diaries hoax of 1983 demonstrated how desperation for historical scoops could override journalistic skepticism, resulting in one of the most expensive and embarrassing media disasters of the 20th century. German magazine *Stern* paid 10 million Deutsche marks for what appeared to be 60 handwritten diaries by Adolf Hitler, discovered in a plane crash in East Germany and smuggled to the West by a mysterious collector. The diaries promised to revolutionize understanding of Nazi history, potentially revealing Hitler's private thoughts and secret plans that historians had never seen.

The forgeries were actually the work of Konrad Kujau, a small-time con artist and Nazi memorabilia dealer who had been producing fake Hitler documents for years. Kujau's technique was remarkably primitive: he used modern paper that hadn't existed during World War II, bound the diaries with postwar materials, and wrote in a script that didn't match Hitler's actual handwriting. The ink contained chemicals that were anachronistic, and the historical content included factual errors that any competent historian should have caught immediately.

Despite these obvious flaws, *Stern's* authentication process was compromised by wishful thinking and competitive pressure. The magazine hired handwriting experts who compared the diary script to other Hitler documents, not realizing that their reference materials were also Kujau forgeries. The historical content seemed plausible because it mostly rehashed information from published sources, with added personal details that made Hitler appear more human and less monstrous than historical records suggested.

The hoax unraveled when forensic scientists tested the paper and ink, immediately revealing that the materials were decades newer than they should have been. The chemical analysis was so conclusive that even *Stern's* most committed believers had to accept that they had been deceived. Kujau was arrested and confessed to the forgeries, explaining that he had never expected the deception to reach such heights of international attention.

The Hitler Diaries scandal destroyed careers, cost millions in legal fees and refunds, and damaged the credibility of historical authentication processes. It revealed how the desire for sensational discoveries could corrupt editorial judgment, leading respected journalists to abandon basic verification procedures in their rush to publish exclusive content. The hoax also demonstrated the enduring public fascination with Hitler and Nazi history, showing how this interest could be exploited by skilled manipulators who understood what audiences wanted to believe about the past.

These hoaxes share common elements that reveal recurring patterns in human credulity: they exploited existing beliefs and desires, leveraged respected authorities to provide credibility, used just enough technical detail to sound legitimate, and succeeded because audiences wanted to believe in extraordinary possibilities.

Chapter 19

Blood, Roses, and Rotten Teeth

The Tudors turned monarchy into performance art, complete with costume changes, dramatic deaths, and enough backstage drama to make reality TV producers weep with envy. This was a dynasty that treated the throne like a director's chair, orchestrating spectacular displays of power while privately nursing festering leg wounds and dental disasters that would make modern orthodontists rich beyond measure.

The Crash That Changed a King

On January 24, 1536, King Henry VIII discovered that gravity applies even to monarchs when he crashed spectacularly at Greenwich Palace's tiltyard, pinned beneath his fully armored horse that weighed over a ton. This wasn't his first rodeo disaster, earlier jousting accidents had already left him with painful ulcers, and in 1524 he nearly lost an eye after forgetting to lower his visor, proving that even kings can forget basic safety equipment. He was knocked unconscious for hours while rumors of his death reached Queen Anne Boleyn, who suffered a miscarriage five days later. The timing was particularly awkward since Henry had just marked Katharine of Aragon's death by wearing yellow mourning attire, apparently mistaking a funeral for a celebration in what might be history's most tone-deaf fashion choice.

The accident marked the transformation from "Bluff King Hal," the jovial Renaissance prince, into the paranoid tyrant of legend. Chronic pain, festering leg wounds, and violent mood swings followed the head trauma, while his waist expanded from 35 inches to over 50 by the 1540s, a progression documented in his surviving armor like a medieval weight-gain timeline. He eventually needed mechanical contraptions to move around, essentially becoming the first monarch to require mobility aids while simultaneously executing people for treason. Before the crash, he was an athlete; afterward, he became the brooding king remembered for gnawing turkey legs at banquets, though that particular image owes more to Hollywood than historical menus.

The Sweet Tooth Queen's Dental Disaster

Queen Elizabeth I adored candied violets and marzipan with the enthusiasm of someone who had never heard of dental hygiene. By the 1590s, her teeth were blackened and decayed from England's booming sugar imports, creating a royal smile that could clear a room faster than a court scandal. The most remarkable part? Ambitious courtiers deliberately blackened their own teeth so the queen wouldn't feel singled out. Nothing says career advancement quite like voluntary dental self-destruction, proving that sucking up to the boss is a timeless art form that occasionally requires actual sacrifice.

Fashion Police, Tudor Edition

Tudor sumptuary laws turned getting dressed into a legal minefield where wearing the wrong fabric could land you in court. Only royalty could sport purple silk, while gold cloth and sable fur were reserved for the upper elite, essentially creating a dress code that made modern country club rules look relaxed. Merchants caught wearing above their station faced fines, transforming fashion into a political statement where your outfit literally declared your loyalty to the social hierarchy. Imagine explaining to a traffic cop that your designer sneakers violated the Constitution.

The Rose-Colored Propaganda King

Henry VII had the weakest claim to the throne in English history, having essentially won it in a raffle called the Battle of Bosworth Field. His solution? Invent the Tudor Rose, a red-and-white hybrid that served as the medieval equivalent of a corporate rebrand after a hostile takeover. This botanical PR campaign appeared on everything from coins to palace walls, essentially gaslighting an entire kingdom into forgetting that their new king's primary qualification was being good with a sword. The propaganda worked so well that people almost forgot the realm was still one bad harvest away from civil war.

Death as Prime-Time Entertainment

Tudor executions were the era's must-see television, combining the spectacle of a gladiator match with the moral authority of a church service. Anne Boleyn's execution broke tradition by being staged privately within the Tower of London with a French swordsman, apparently even royal beheadings needed international flair. Meanwhile, Thomas More quipped to his executioner, "See me safe up, for my coming down I can shift for myself," proving that gallows humor was literally invented at the gallows. Vendors sold pies, children scrambled for good views, and the condemned were expected to deliver final lines worthy of Shakespeare, turning judicial murder into performance art.

The Palace-Building Addict

Henry VIII collected palaces like a modern billionaire collects yachts, except with more gold leaf and fewer helicopter pads. This wasn't mere royal retail therapy, it was a calculated strategy wrapped in architectural magnificence. Henry didn't just own palaces; he possessed over 60 properties and transformed places like Hampton Court into sprawling complexes with over a thousand rooms, creating what amounted to small cities dedicated entirely to his comfort and political theater.

The genius lay in the constant movement. By making the court a perpetually traveling circus, Henry kept his nobles in his direct presence, preventing them from forming independent power bases in their own territories. It's the medieval equivalent of a CEO requiring all executives to work from headquarters rather than remote offices, except the headquarters kept changing locations and required you to pack your entire wardrobe in ox-drawn carts. The logistics alone must have been nightmarish, with hundreds of courtiers, servants, furniture, tapestries, and even royal toilet seats constantly relocating across England like a luxury nomadic tribe.

Henry's most audacious display was the "Field of the Cloth of Gold" in 1520, where he constructed an entire temporary palace from scratch just for a single meeting with the French king. This prefabricated wonder was pure theater, designed to demonstrate that English wealth was so abundant they could literally build disposable palaces for diplomatic small talk. The extravagance was so over-the-top that both kings nearly bankrupted their treasuries trying to out-magnificence each other, proving that international dick-measuring contests were alive and well five centuries before social media made them a daily occurrence.

The psychological driver behind Henry's building obsession reveals something deeply human about power and insecurity. Like any modern person who stress-shops or renovates their kitchen during a midlife crisis, Henry was essentially using construction as therapy, except his therapy projects could house small armies and required parliamentary funding. Each new palace was a monument to his authority, but also a distraction from the growing problems of religious reform, marital disasters, and the nagging reality that even absolute monarchs can't build their way out of existential anxiety.

Bloody Mary's PR Problem

Mary Tudor earned her infamous nickname not just from executing hundreds of Protestants, but from having the historical equivalent of terrible publicists. Protestant writers like John Foxe turned her into the poster child for religious extremism in his bestselling Acts and Monuments, cementing a reputation that outlasted her actual reign. While her burnings were genuinely brutal, she wasn't uniquely bloodthirsty by 16th-century standards, she just drew the short straw in the propaganda wars that followed.

The Virgin Queen's Marriage Scam

Elizabeth I weaponized her single status like a diplomatic nuclear option, dangling marriage prospects to foreign princes while having zero intention of actually saying "I do." Royal marriages were treaties with wedding dresses, not romantic comedies, and Elizabeth understood that keeping suitors waiting was more powerful than any actual alliance. She turned virginity into a brand identity while using romance as foreign policy, proving that sometimes the best relationship strategy is never committing to anyone.

Cosmic Politics and Royal Horoscopes

Tudor monarchs consulted astrologers like modern politicians hire pollsters, except with more robes, mystical charts, and significantly less scientific methodology. Elizabeth I treated John Dee like a cabinet minister who happened to specialize in planetary alignments rather than fiscal policy, consulting him on everything from coronation dates to military strategy. Dee wasn't just some street-corner fortune teller, he was a brilliant mathematician, cartographer, and scholar who advised the queen on navigation routes for explorers while simultaneously calculating the most auspicious times for state decisions based on celestial movements. The line between science and superstition was so blurred that England's greatest minds saw no contradiction in using advanced mathematics to chart the stars while believing those same stars controlled human destiny.

The psychological appeal of astrology in Tudor times reveals something deeply relatable about human nature and our eternal struggle with uncertainty. In an era when plague could wipe out entire neighborhoods, harvests failed without warning, and political alliances shifted like weather patterns, astrology offered the illusion of predictability in an unpredictable world. It's the same impulse that makes modern people check their horoscopes during stressful periods or obsessively refresh weather apps during hurricane season, we desperately want to believe that someone, somewhere, has figured out the pattern behind the chaos. Henry VII, whose claim to the throne was shakier than a house of cards in a windstorm, particularly relied on soothsayers to provide cosmic justification for his rule, essentially hiring the medieval equivalent of a PR firm that specialized in divine endorsements.

Even ordinary Londoners lived by astrological guidance, blaming bad harvests and plagues on cosmic events while astrologers operated like medieval Amazon, always having another "essential" magical book conveniently available for purchase. The city buzzed with fortune tellers, almanac sellers, and cosmic consultants who could explain why your business failed (Mercury was in retrograde) or why your marriage was rocky (Venus was poorly aspected), creating an entire economy built on anxiety and the human need for explanations. The irony is that while Tudor England was experiencing unprecedented scientific advances in navigation, medicine, and engineering, people still preferred mystical explanations for daily life, proving that even in the Renaissance, many folks would rather blame the stars than take responsibility for their problems.

Dining Above the Salt

Tudor banquets turned food into social mapping, where your distance from the salt cellar determined your worth as a human being. Henry VIII's court feasted on roasted peacocks and swan while peasants survived on pottage, essentially medieval gruel with aspirations. The phrase "above the salt" literally meant you mattered; "below the salt" meant you were decorative furniture with digestive systems. Dinner wasn't just a meal, it was hierarchy served on a plate, proving that even seasoning could be a status symbol in a world where everything from your clothing to your lunch announced your place in the cosmic pecking order.

Chapter 20

Humanity's Legal Drug Habit

If history is a play, caffeine is the understudy who hijacked the show, jittering across stage in a doublet of nerves and triumph. From coffeehouses buzzing with rumors to teacups clinking through empire-building, this humble stimulant rewired civilization one sleepless night at a time. Forget steam engines or silicon chips, the real power surge came from a bean, a leaf, and a billion humans insisting, "I'll just have one more."

The Goat That Started It All

Legend says a goat herder named Kaldi in 9th-century Ethiopia noticed his flock bouncing about like they'd discovered techno music eight centuries early. The goats weren't just frisky, they were performing what can only be described as parkour after nibbling on crimson berries. Kaldi, equal parts baffled and curious, gathered the berries and carried them to nearby Sufi monks, who brewed them into a dark liquid that kept them alert through marathon prayer sessions. Instead of nodding off mid-recitation, they found themselves chanting with the enthusiasm of overcaffeinated cheerleaders.

Whether Kaldi existed or represents Ethiopian storytelling at its finest remains charmingly unclear. What we do know is that coffee originated in the Ethiopian highlands, where wild *Coffea arabica* plants grew naturally. The plant's bright red cherries contained seeds packed with caffeine as a natural pesticide. This evolutionary defense mechanism against insects would eventually become humanity's favorite vice.

The Ethiopian coffee ceremony, still practiced today across the country, transforms brewing into a three-hour ritual of community bonding. The hostess roasts green beans over an open flame, filling the room with aromatic smoke while incense burns nearby. The beans are ground by hand, brewed in a clay pot called a *jebena*, and served in three rounds, *abol* (first), *tona* (second), and *baraka* (third, meaning "blessing"). Each round grows progressively weaker, but the conversation grows stronger. It's democracy in miniature, everyone gets a voice, everyone shares the same cup rotation, and everyone leaves slightly more awake than they arrived.

This ceremony reveals something profound. Coffee never was just about the buzz, it was about slowing time enough to connect with other humans while simultaneously speeding up your heartbeat. The contradiction would follow caffeine through every culture it conquered.

Coffeehouses Are the Internet Before the Internet

By the 1600s, London's coffeehouses had become humanity's first attempt at social networking, minus the algorithm but with considerably more shouting. These establishments, dubbed "penny universities" by their patrons, offered intellectual stimulation and heated debates for the cost of a single coin, roughly equivalent to buying knowledge by the cup. Lloyd's of London, now a global insurance powerhouse, began when Edward Lloyd started serving coffee and posting shipping news on his coffeehouse walls. Merchants would gather to assess maritime risks over steaming mugs, essentially inventing modern insurance while caffeinated.

The physical layout of these spaces encouraged democracy through proximity. Long communal tables meant strangers sat elbow-to-elbow, while the proprietor often read newspapers aloud to the illiterate. Coffee, imported from the Ottoman Empire, cost about the same as a pint of ale but delivered alertness instead of drowsiness, a revolutionary trade-off that extended productive hours well into the evening.

These coffeehouses terrified authorities precisely because they democratized information. In 1675, King Charles II attempted to ban them, calling them "seminaries of sedition" where "false news is devised and spread." The public outcry forced him to rescind the proclamation within days. Coffee had already rewired London's social fabric so thoroughly that banning it would have been like attempting to uninvent conversation itself.

The parallel to modern social media is uncanny, both created spaces where strangers could debate, gossip, and share information at unprecedented speed. The main difference? Coffeehouse arguments occasionally led to duels rather than blocking someone on Twitter. Also, you had to actually leave your house.

Espresso Gets Italy Legally Lightning

In 1901, Luigi Bezzera unveiled his espresso machine at the Milan Fair, creating what amounted to a steam-powered coffee cannon. The word "espresso" means "pressed out" or "express", referring both to the pressurized brewing method and the speed of service. Bezzera's machine used steam pressure to force hot water through finely ground coffee in under 30 seconds, producing a concentrated shot topped with *crema*, the golden foam that became espresso's signature.

Italian espresso culture developed its own rigid etiquette. No cappuccinos after 11 AM (the milk was considered too heavy for afternoon digestion), no sitting at the bar (standing encouraged quick consumption), and absolutely no ordering a "large espresso" (an oxymoron that could get you deported). The typical Italian consumed their espresso in three sips while standing, paid their few lire, and continued their day properly caffeinated.

Espresso machines became the steam engines of Italian culture, installed in every corner café and treated with mechanical reverence. The barista's skill in grinding, tamping, and extracting became a craft requiring years of apprenticeship. A perfect espresso shot demanded precisely 7-9 grams of coffee, extracted in 20-30 seconds at 190-196°F, producing 1.5 ounces of liquid with a thick crema layer. Getting any variable wrong resulted in coffee that was either bitter, sour, weak, or burnt, and Italian customers were not shy about expressing their disappointment.

This obsession with precision would later drive American coffee culture completely insane. Starbucks took the Italian espresso concept and supersized it into 20-ounce sugar bombs that would make a Neapolitan barista weep into his perfectly measured shot.

Soda's Sweet Deception

Dr. John Stith Pemberton invented Coca-Cola in 1886 as a patent medicine, originally including cocaine from coca leaves and caffeine from kola nuts. The cocaine disappeared by 1903 due to public health concerns, but the caffeine remained as the secret hook that kept customers returning. Pemberton's bookkeeper, Frank Robinson, coined the name and designed the distinctive Spencerian script logo that remains unchanged today.

Early soda marketing focused on medicinal benefits, Coca-Cola promised to cure headaches, while Pepsi-Cola (1893) marketed itself as a digestive aid. The reality was simpler. Caffeine provided a mild stimulant effect, sugar delivered quick energy, and carbonation created a festive sensation that made the whole experience feel celebratory rather than medicinal.

By the 1950s, soda companies had discovered that caffeine addiction was excellent for business. The average 12-ounce cola contained 34mg of caffeine, enough to create physical dependence with regular consumption but not enough to cause obvious jitters. Supermarkets became battlegrounds where sugar-buzzed children ricocheted between aisles like caffeinated pinballs, while parents learned to shop with the efficiency of hostage negotiators.

The psychology was brilliant. Associate caffeine with fun, fizz, and flavoring, and customers would consume their daily dose without thinking of it as a drug habit. Coca-Cola's secret formula remains locked in an Atlanta vault, but the real secret was never the recipe, it was training the world to crave caffeine three times a day without realizing it.

Energy Drinks Become Liquid Productivity

Red Bull launched in Austria in 1987, adapting a Thai energy tonic called *Krating Daeng* for Western palates. The original Thai formula contained 50mg of caffeine per 8.4-ounce can, plus taurine (an amino acid), B-vitamins, and enough sugar to power a small aircraft. Austrian entrepreneur Dietrich Mateschitz discovered the drink during a business trip to Thailand, where it allegedly cured his jet lag, and partnered with the original creator to modify the formula for global distribution.

The marketing strategy was genius. Instead of competing with coffee or soda, Red Bull positioned itself as liquid performance enhancement. The brand sponsored extreme sports, created its own media company, and marketed directly to exhausted students, overworked professionals, and anyone attempting to squeeze 28 hours of productivity from a 24-hour day. The slogan "Red Bull gives you wings" wasn't literal, but it captured something real, the feeling of synthetic energy when your natural reserves had been depleted.

Modern energy drinks contain 80-300mg of caffeine per serving, often combined with taurine, guarana (another caffeine source), ginseng, and enough sugar to trigger insulin spikes visible from space. The most potent varieties pack more caffeine than three cups of coffee, creating a stimulant experience so intense that some countries have banned their sale to minors.

The cultural shift was significant. Coffee had been social, tea had been contemplative, but energy drinks were purely utilitarian. They represented caffeine stripped of ritual, community, and pleasure, just chemical efficiency in an aluminum can. The rise of energy drinks coincided with the gig economy, 24-hour work cultures, and the general acceleration of modern life. When society demanded more productivity than human biology could provide, energy drinks offered a chemical solution packaged like a soft drink.

The Neuroscience of Need

Adenosine is your brain's internal sleep timer, building up throughout the day and binding to receptors that gradually slow neural activity. Caffeine's molecular structure mimics adenosine closely enough to slip into the same receptors, but instead of slowing brain activity, it blocks the sleepiness signal entirely. Meanwhile, adenosine continues accumulating in your bloodstream, creating what neuroscientists call "sleep debt."

Just think your brain as a nightclub with adenosine as the bouncer slowly dimming the lights and encouraging everyone to go home. Caffeine shows up with fake ID, takes the bouncer's place, and keeps the party going while the real bouncer pounds on the door outside. Eventually, that bouncer is going to get back in, and he's going to be very, very angry.

The effect cascades through multiple neurotransmitter systems. Blocked adenosine receptors trigger dopamine release (creating mild euphoria), increase norepinephrine production (improving focus), and enhance acetylcholine activity (boosting memory formation). This neurochemical symphony explains why that first cup of coffee doesn't just wake you up, it makes you feel optimistic, focused, and capable of conquering the day.

Tolerance develops as your brain produces more adenosine receptors to compensate for caffeine's interference. Within a week of regular consumption, you need increasing amounts of caffeine just to feel normal, while the original euphoric effects diminish. Withdrawal symptoms, headaches, irritability, fatigue, and difficulty concentrating, result from adenosine flooding receptors that had grown accustomed to caffeine's blockade.

The half-life of caffeine is 5-6 hours, meaning a cup of coffee consumed at 2 PM still has 25% of its caffeine circulating at bedtime. This explains the modern epidemic of sleep disorders among heavy coffee drinkers who insist caffeine "doesn't affect" their sleep. It does, they've simply forgotten what natural sleep feels like.

Politics in a Porcelain Cup

Coffee and tea didn't just fuel empires, they financed them. European colonial powers built entire economies around caffeinated crops. Dutch plantations in Java and Ceylon, British tea gardens in India and Ceylon, French coffee cultivation in Vietnam and Haiti. The human cost was staggering, with millions of indigenous workers and enslaved people dying to satisfy European caffeine addictions.

The Boston Tea Party wasn't just about taxation, it was about corporate monopolies and economic sovereignty. Similar dynamics play out today as coffee farmers in developing countries receive a fraction of the price paid by consumers in wealthy nations, while multinational corporations capture most of the profits. Fair trade certification attempts to address these inequities, but the fundamental power imbalance remains. Poor countries grow the crops, rich countries control the brands.

Modern governments face a fascinating contradiction, they tax caffeine-laden products while depending on caffeinated citizens to maintain economic productivity. Politicians routinely campaign on coffee shop stages, recognizing that caffeine has become democracy's unofficial fuel. Congressional hearings run on coffee, Supreme Court justices start each day with caffeine, and virtually every major policy decision is made by people running on chemical stimulation.

The regulatory approach varies wildly by country. While some nations restrict energy drink sales to minors, others treat caffeine as completely benign. This inconsistency reflects caffeine's unique status as the world's only universally legal psychoactive drug that also happens to increase worker productivity. No government wants to ban a substance that makes their workforce more efficient, even if that same substance is technically addictive.

The Ritual Psychology of Stimulation

The power of caffeine transcends its chemical effects through ritual reinforcement. The morning coffee routine becomes a psychological anchor, grinding beans, boiling water, inhaling the aroma, taking that first transformative sip. These actions trigger conditioned responses that begin the stimulant effect before the caffeine hits your bloodstream.

Pavlov would have been fascinated by modern coffee culture. The hiss of an espresso machine becomes an auditory cue for alertness, the sight of a familiar café logo triggers anticipatory energy, and even the act of holding a warm mug can improve mood and social warmth. Coffee shops exploit these psychological associations with carefully designed soundscapes, lighting schemes, and aromatic environments that maximize the perceived effect of their products.

The social dimensions matter equally. Offering someone coffee signals hospitality and creates shared experience. "Coffee dates" provide socially acceptable excuses for extended conversation, while "coffee breaks" legitimize workplace rest periods. In many cultures, refusing offered coffee or tea represents serious social rejection, caffeine has become the universal gesture of human connection.

Energy drinks operate differently, stripping away ritual and community in favor of pure efficiency. The can design, marketing imagery, and consumption context all emphasize individual performance over social bonding. It's caffeine as software optimization rather than cultural practice. You don't sip an energy drink contemplatively, you slam it like you're loading ammunition into your nervous system.

Thank You

So, there you go. You've marched through dictators who rewrote reality, eaten your way across death-by-dinner menus, watched your bones dissolve in space, and seen rockstars survive more chaos than most civilizations. If you're still standing, congrats, you're officially the kind of person who can't be killed by trivia.

But don't get too smug. The world's full of facts waiting to trip you up at the next family quiz night, pub showdown, or awkward dinner conversation. Remember: somewhere out there, someone's uncle is already Googling obscure Roman plumbing just to ruin your moment of glory.

Take these stories, throw them around, argue with them, claim you knew them all along. Because that's the point, trivia isn't just about knowing, it's about swaggering into the room with the confidence of a dictator in sunglasses, or an author convinced rotten apples are a muse.

And if anyone calls you out for being a know-it-all? Just smile, sip your coffee (maybe not 50 cups of it), and say: *"Actually..."*

Want more trivia, wild history stories, and quizzes that keep your brain buzzing?

Scan the QR code below and join our FREE weekly newsletter.

You'll get:

- Fresh quizzes straight to your inbox.
- Strange-but-true history stories.
- Fun facts that didn't fit in this book (we had *too many*).
- Sneak previews of upcoming releases.

As a bonus, you'll also get an exclusive excerpt from our Amazon #1 Bestseller:

Shut the Fact Up, the book that proves truth is stranger (and funnier) than fiction.

Printed in Dunstable, United Kingdom